ETIQUETTE

a guide to
modern manners

ETIQUETTE

Henry Russell

CASSELL
ILLUSTRATED

To my enemies

(*My friends already know all this*)

" *Qu'on ne dise pas que je n'ai rien dit de nouveau:
la disposition des matières est nouvelle.* "

Pascal

The author wishes to thank the following for their help and suggestions:
*Sara Jones, Jon Asbury, Jack Angell, Mark Fletcher,
Brian Innes, Vanna Motto, Aruna Vasudevan.*

First published in Great Britain in 2006 by Cassell Illustrated, a division of
Octopus Publishing Group Limited, 2-4 Heron Quays, London E14 4JP

Text copyright © 2006 Henry Russell
Design and layout © 2006 Cassell Illustrated
Illustrations by Emma Parrish
Designed by Geoff Borin

A CIP catalogue record for this book is available from the British Library.

ISBN-13: 978-1-844035-38-0
ISBN-10: 1-844035-38-7

10 9 8 7 6 5 4 3 2 1

Printed in China

CONTENTS

INTRODUCTION

―――――――――――――――― ❧ ――――――――――――――――

> " Never speak disrespectfully of Society....
> Only people who can't get into it do that. "
>
> Oscar Wilde, *The Importance of Being Earnest*

Everyone wonders what to do for the best. Sometimes the questions raised are moral, and in extreme cases the wrong moral decisions can lead to serious trouble. However, most of the problems we routinely encounter are rather less weighty. They are largely matters of what constitutes the right social behaviour – what to say and when to say it, whether or not to wear a tie to the office party, whether to call the children's teacher 'Mr Smith' or 'John'.

These are problems of etiquette. Etiquette receives less consideration than morality because violations are seldom harmful, just embarrassing. Moral misdemeanours, in contrast, can lead to imprisonment or death.

Not all questions of etiquette are entirely trivial. People are usually at pains to ensure that their comments do not cause unnecessary offence to others; they tend to become most anxious when they have to participate in rites of passage, especially christenings, marriages and funerals. As Walter Savage Landor wrote, 'More can be said in a minute than can be forgotten in a lifetime'.

Nevertheless, with certain exceptions, it is quite proper that most niceties of etiquette should be taken less than completely seriously. A man who blanks someone because he has asked him the location of the 'toilet' instead of using his own preferred genteelism for WC is an ass, tout court. While we may deprecate those who say 'sweet' instead of 'pudding', their transgression would not be serious even if there were a law against it.

There was a time when such things mattered more than they do today. Throughout the 18th and 19th centuries, and for the greater part of the 20th century, the observance of etiquette was both a diversion and an occupation, especially for women. More and more rituals were devised to create a sense of exclusivity among initiates. These rituals were later codified and to some extent invented by writers of all sexes. Leaders of fashion and soi-disant pundits pontificated on the rights and wrongs of dress, cutlery and a host of related trivia. An individual's acceptability in society and, indeed, his entire reputation might have hung not upon his honesty, but upon how he conveyed his soup from bowl to mouth.

In the United States, Emily Post laid down the rules of social behaviour in *Etiquette: The Blue Book of Social Usage*. First published in 1922, revised editions appeared regularly for more than 30 years. Among other prominent standard setters were Amy Vanderbilt, and Eleanor Roosevelt in her *Book of Common Sense Etiquette* (1962).

Prescriptive etiquette reached its nadir in Britain in 1956 with *Noblesse Oblige: An Enquiry into the Identifiable Characteristics of the English Aristocracy*, an anthology best remembered for dividing social behaviour into two categories: 'upper class' ('U') and 'non-upper class' ('non-U'). The former was extolled and the latter deplored. The social impact of this absurd book, edited by Nancy Mitford, may still be felt today: there are, almost incredibly, some circles in which the use of the supposedly 'non-U' term 'serviette' instead of the supposedly 'U' term 'napkin' would still arouse adverse comment, and from which anyone using the 'wrong' term might find himself excluded.

Most people who live by the precepts of Mitford have now been sidelined, and modern society is better equipped than ever before to keep etiquette in proper perspective. There are several reasons for this healthy development. One is that women are now freer, if not actually liberated, and have more important – or at least more pressing – matters to occupy them. Another is the 'anything goes' spirit of the age. There has lately been a welcome rehabilitation of Rabelais' maxim *fay ce que vouldras* (do what you will), which was vilified in the middle of the 20th century as the watchword of a black magician called Aleister Crowley.

Children of the sixties then brought it back into favour with the sensible rider 'as long as it doesn't harm anyone else'.

There are those who believe that this zeitgeist has made etiquette rule books redundant. Towards the end of 1995, the London *Evening Standard* newspaper boldly announced that 'Today…no general etiquette survives, whether of clothes, of speech, or of behaviour. Socially, life is a journey without maps. Only style choices remain, and good and bad manners'.

But there still are many occasions when we are uncertain of what to do, what to wear, what to say and how to say it. This uncertainty undermines us. The most elaborate premeditated attempts to behave properly may go unnoticed, while the smallest departure from generally accepted standards of behaviour arouses derision. Dire offence may spring from the most trivial causes. If, for example, a man eats peas off his knife, the 'victim' (if that is not too strong a term to describe someone who happens to have witnessed the petty outrage) may feel aesthetic revulsion; the 'culprit', meanwhile, may grow ill-disposed towards the person in front of whom he feels he has made a fool of himself, on La Rochefoucauld's principle that 'We may forgive those who hurt us, but never those whom we hurt'.

The only serious reason for observing etiquette is to avoid upsetting others. Etiquette is not, or shouldn't be, a weapon in the class struggle, a stick with which to beat those of whom you happen not to like the look or sound. This book gives an outline of what other people expect – not in the sense of 'England expects', but in the sense of 'presumes most likely to occur'.

Readers will avoid embarrassment in their social intercourse only if they treat the information contained here, not as the laws of the Medes and the Persians, but as reportage of current conventions – conventions which they can observe or flout as they prefer.

If you do something outré unintentionally, onlookers' gasps of astonishment may throw you off your stride; if, on the other hand, you know that your flies are undone and you have left them open deliberately in order to shock or to draw attention to yourself, you may be looked upon not as provincial or beyond the pale but as a style guru. In the words of the Trummy Young / Sy Oliver song, ''T ain't what you do, it's the way that you do it'. Still, while iconoclasts make their own rules, most of us prefer to familiarise ourselves with established conventions and stick to them.

The purpose of good behaviour is to make everyone – yourself and those around you – feel at ease. And what, as Norman Douglas asked, are good manners but the outward expression of kindliness? And what is kindliness but common sense?

Henry Russell

GENERAL
BEHAVIOUR

Just as some people can't face the evening without a stiffener, there are others who cannot engage in any form of social intercourse or business without a preconceived schema of what they're going to say and what indeed they are going to endeavour to avoid mentioning. This book is not on the whole prescriptive: what follows are mostly suggestions, not instructions; the occasional use of the imperative mood is merely *façon de parler*. It stakes various premises, but acknowledges that we live in a pluralistic society. The reader may care to venerate its tenets as holy writ, or alternatively do the opposite of everything it suggests. If you find it diverting it will have achieved its modest purpose.

CONVERSATION

" Questioning is not the mode of conversation among gentlemen. "

Samuel Johnson, *Boswell's Life*

If we go by what we read, we are not supposed to discuss politics, money, religion or sex in polite company. Which leaves art, and since no one knows anything about that, what are we left with? Nothing. If in doubt, let the host and hostess be responsible for setting the tone, and take it from there. If you are running the show, start off as trivially and uncontroversially as you can and see what develops.

Remember that it is bad form to leave someone standing on his own, and it is reprehensible to leave someone all evening with a known bore (or then again, perhaps not). If you find that you're frequently left with bores all night, either you're going to the wrong parties or you're a bore yourself.

Some etiquette authorities proscribe talking about one's own work and asking other people about theirs. Some quote Wilde, 'It is very vulgar to talk about one's business. Only people like stock brokers do that, and then merely at dinner parties'. But this is a line in *The Importance of Being Earnest*, not a Mosaic Law. 'What do you do?' is likewise frowned upon and regarded as contemptibly trite, but generally what else is there to say?

If you use this line, you must be prepared for all the possible answers. A 19-year-old male friend addressed it to a lady in a short skirt and fishnet tights as she sat on a Soho bar-stool. To which the answer was vouchsafed: 'I work, like everybody else'.

You may be able to carry it off, if you say it in a mildly ironic tone meant to convey your awareness that, although it's a corny line, contrived situations call for contrived measures. As a halfway house, you could modify it to 'What are you doing at the moment?'

One not-too-leaden way to start a conversation with someone you don't know is to talk about an external event or phenomenon about which he might also have an opinion: the difficulty of finding the venue; the traffic en route; a painting on the wall. You might even open with the weather, but only if it is extreme and you are desperate. Asking the other person how he knows the host is not a bad opening gambit. In any case, remember that you are supposed to be introducing a light topic for discussion, not trying to sustain a soliloquy until the dinner gong is sounded. Conversation is to some extent like tennis – when you are serving, if the first ball is not returned, put another one in play. (But don't stretch the metaphor too far…for every ace you lose a point.) Monologue meanwhile is a timeless Test: no one wants it and paradoxically it never produces a result.

Some common replies to 'What do you do?' require quick thinking on the part of the interlocutor to avoid a frosty ensuing silence. They include: 'Not a lot', 'Housewife', 'Chartered accountant' and 'Actuary'. Forewarned is forearmed, so think of a suave riposte to each.

You can always break the ice by being controversial, but this takes courage and skill. You must ensure that you're not being inflammatory and you must never be tactless.

" *The question 'What do you do?' means 'How do you earn your living?'*
On my passport I am described as a 'Writer'; this is not embarrassing for me
in dealing with the authorities, because immigration and customs officials know
that some kinds of writers make lots of money. But if a stranger in the train
asks me my occupation, I never answer 'writer' for fear that he may go on to
ask me what I write, and to answer 'poetry' would embarrass us both, for we
both know that nobody can earn a living simply by writing poetry.

(The most satisfactory answer I have discovered, satisfactory
because it withers curiosity, is to say Medieval Historian.) "

W.H. Auden, *The Dyer's Hand*

Never be deterred from saying something on the grounds that everyone will have heard it already, and never think no one will be interested in little old me. Remember the epigraph of this book: '*Qu'on ne dise pas que je n'ai rien dit de nouveau: la disposition des matières est nouvelle*'. (Let no one say that I have said nothing new: the arrangement of the material is new.) If you are truly polite you will always be too busy thinking of others to have any time to be inhibited by your own self-consciousness.

" Although there exist many thousand subjects for elegant conversation, there are persons who cannot meet a cripple without talking about feet. "

Ernest Bramah, *The Wallet of Kai Lung*

AGE

Never ask someone else's, and never ask others to guess yours. If you are asked to guess someone else's, it is politic to subtract at least five years from what you really think, unless you have been asked to guess by a teenager, in which case it is advisable to add a year or two. Under-tens are impressed only if you get their age exactly right.

BETTING

There is no such thing as a dull subject, and in the hands of a good narrator both the theory and practice of betting may be riveting. Many people, however, make the mistake of expecting the audience to believe that they have come out ahead over a lifetime. Few habitual gamblers are net winners: those who tell you they have 'won' the National Lottery have almost certainly excised from their account the dozen losing tickets that put them out of pocket overall.

BORES

**“*A bore is a man who, when asked how he is,*
tells you. ”**

English Proverb

If someone is about to tell you an anecdote for the fiftieth time, you might try to put him off by saying 'Yes, that's a lovely story', but even if you're brave enough to do that, you may still not be able to stop him: bores are nearly always indefatigable and usually cannot be deflected, even if the audience is rude enough to draw attention to their dullness.

You may choose to pretend that it is you who are boring them. Robert Browning is said to have concluded an audience with a tedious admirer of his work with: 'But my dear fellow, this is too bad. I am monopolising you'. An Oxford don (now deceased) once dismissed a brace of bores (one of whom – let's start off as honestly as we hope to continue – was me) from his presence with: 'But I mustn't take up any more of your time'. (Note the exact words: 'valuable time' would have been obviously and unchivalrously disparaging.)

Such gambits are witty but risk giving offence, and since perfectly civilised people will always avoid causing pain or embarrassment to others – even at the risk of hurting themselves – the best advice is probably that, if ennui is inevitable, lie back and…well, if not actually enjoy it, at least put a brave face on it. You can either politely not listen or – if you've heard the same story from the same person before – study the fascinating variations in detail that bores often permit themselves on these occasions. Then again, if it's a well-rehearsed bore you're enduring, you can marvel at his incredible consistency.

> "*Every hero becomes a bore at last.*"

Ralph Waldo Emerson, *Representative Men. Uses of Great Men*

SOCIAL SITUATION

You are a bore. Someone asks you if you have ever been to Bali.
You have not. How should you respond?

Along the lines of: 'I nearly did. I cleared the dates at work then spent an evening looking at low fare carriers online and eventually found this amazing deal that only costs £245 return from East Midlands if you travel on a Wednesday and your stay includes a Saturday night. The outward flight goes via Gdansk and Vladikavkaz, and there's a four-hour stopover in Mumbai, but it's still a considerable saving on the scheduled airlines, even if you live in Cornwall like I do. BA is typically over a grand return even in coach and Lufthansa is still more expensive but I wouldn't fly with them anyway because they use Frankfurt as a hub and that's the most disgusting airport on the face of the planet… but then there was the nightclub bombing so I thought I'm not going there no way José I'll go back to La Gomera like last year…'.

COMPLIMENTS

Compliments used to be regarded as rude, but nowadays they are quite in order as long as there is neither a hint of equivocation, nor the possibility that they will subsequently be interpreted as ambivalent. English playwright Alan Bennett took the view that – so numerous are the pitfalls – the only thing you can possibly say to the cast backstage after a performance is 'Marvellous, marvellous, marvellous'. If you pay compliments that can be construed as backhanded, don't be surprised when they are.

If you're going to praise, praise everything – don't play the Cordelia, because if you do it may be interpreted as an implicit criticism of something else you haven't mentioned. Thus for example, it may be advisable to thank your hostess for a wonderful evening: if you say it was a lovely meal, it may be taken to suggest that you didn't like the wine or the company.

PERSONAL QUESTIONS

In addition to 'How old are you?' and 'What do you do?' it is wise to avoid 'Was it anything serious?' And for the same reason: the answer may be embarrassing. That goes *a fortiori* for 'How much do you earn?' While it may be amusing and sometimes instructive to ask that straight out (some people affect disgust at those who evade giving a response), there are good reasons for not raising such a sensitive subject. First, the most likely reply is either 'Mind your own business' or the demurely veiled alternative 'I'm not telling you that' with any degree of emphasis you like on the objective and/or the demonstrative pronoun. Neither encourages further discourse. If the question happens to evoke a numerical response the conversation has drifted into a dangerous reach. The sum of money mentioned will probably be incredible: if you earn that much, how come you drive only a budget car; if you earn so little, how come you have a holiday home on Cap Ferrat? As they say in American sitcoms: don't go there.

SOCIAL SITUATION

In conversation at a party someone tells you that he admires Monet's *Water Lilies*. How should you respond?

A) Ask him if he loves the work because he wishes he could paint that well himself.

B) Suggest that he is psychologically debilitated by the realisation that he will never create anything as good.

C) Tell him your own response to the work, or say something witty and/or interesting about the artist, or bring the subject round to another topic about which you know something.

(c) Why do people assume that appreciation of art is a reflection of the personality of the observer? One of art's main attractions is that it is apart from the self.

HOW DO YOU LIKE IT HERE?

If people ask you this, bear in mind they may be natives. If they are, it is certain that they want you to gush. So that's what you should do, particularly in New York and Tel Aviv, every native of which seems to think he hewed his birthplace from the living rock himself. So even if you've just been mugged on the Subway or spent five hours at an army checkpoint, say what you can.

I was once asked that question by a Frankfurter, and although my private view was that the city on the Main is not the most immediately admirable jewel in the crown of industrial Germany, I replied that I thought it was lovely. I really wished that my interlocutor had left it at that, but she persisted: 'In what way? What do you particularly like about it?' I said there was nothing at which I could shake a stick, just a feeling. Still not off the hook, I told her that it reminded me of Geneva.

She looked happy, but not satisfied. 'How is it like Geneva?' I had no option but to tell her that to my mind the link was that they both had a lot of banks. She is one of several people who will flit through the pages of this book with whom I have not since maintained a vigorous correspondence.

Most Britons know that the climate of their native land is inferior to (or at least less sunny than) that of many other countries. They are internationally renowned (not without justification) for speaking among themselves of little other than the ambient meteorological conditions. Yet some of them felt insulted in September 2005 when cricketer Kevin Pietersen told a radio reporter that he'd rather be in Australia because the weather there was much nicer. It wasn't that they didn't see the point – they may even have taken it – it was the fact that, although he plays for England he is – and sounds like – a South African. Often it isn't what's said that causes offence, it's who says it, and when, and how.

Henry: 'This stunning metropolis makes ancient Samarkland look like a dorp.'
Native companion: 'Is that the best you can do?'

GREAT QUESTIONS OF OUR TIME

In 1978 British broadcaster David Frost conducted a series of interviews with Richard M. Nixon. Frost later recalled that, on resuming recording after a break in the schedule, the first thing Nixon said to him was: 'Did you do any fornicating at the weekend?' Despite the authority of (former, disgraced) presidential usage, such questions should not be asked: indeed, it would have been better not to speak at all.

QUOTATIONS

These should be used only when they are fully relevant in context; otherwise they sound like something you prepared before you came out and were going to use come Hell or High Water. And, of course, it's important to be word perfect lest a pedant (which may be defined as any person with a higher standard of accuracy than oneself) put you right.

" *'When a book and a head come into contact and one of them sounds hollow, is it always the book?'*

'Schopenhaeur's line, isn't it?'

'Yes, but it is easier to write a line than to remember it at the perfect moment.' "

Ben Hecht and Charles MacArthur, *The Scoundrel*

PERSONAL CRITICISM

If you make disparaging remarks about A to B, what confidence can B have that you won't say the same things about him to C? On the other hand, if you don't stake any premises, conversation is impossible. You may be able to convey disapproval in honeyed terms but it takes work to achieve.

LITERARY CRITICISM

If you're going to talk about literature, feel free, but avoid at all costs the following words and expressions:

It's effective

Riffing on themes of biography (or anything else)
(© Robert McCrum)

Ballsy high-octane prose (© John Walsh)

Acute reckoning of the small change
of human interaction (© Hugo Barnacle)

The human condition

It works on several levels

Definitive statement of the relation of art to life

Evocative

Objective correlative

Weltanschaaung

X MARKS THE SPOT

Don't ask people directly how they intend to vote or have voted in a political election: in the civilised world the ballot is secret and their choice is between them and their conscience.

MONEY

People who know how to behave in the presence of money – their own or anyone else's – hold the master key to etiquette and success. Saint Paul, despite devoting his life to disputation and courting controversy, managed in his writings to express some ideas with which it is hard to disagree. Among his least contentious statements was that:

" The love of money is the root of all evil. "

(First Epistle to Timothy, 6:10).

BORROWING AND LENDING

" Life, they say, is give and take. Why never take? "

Norman Douglas, *Looking Back*

'Neither a borrower nor a lender be' comes from *Hamlet*, and it is such good advice that it is one of the abiding mysteries of drama in performance that Polonius, who says the line, should almost always be portrayed as a bore, if not as a bore and a buffoon.

Borrowing is best avoided because it can place intolerable strain on a relationship. As Henry de Monthérlant wrote: 'It is when you wish for nothing that you will become the reflection of God'. If you must borrow, try not to ask for anything that you wouldn't lend if it were yours.

Although many people display books on shelves in the common parts of their homes, guests should be at pains to remember that, despite any appearances to the contrary, they are not in a lending library. If you are sufficiently interested in a book to want to borrow it, you will be sufficiently interested to find a copy for yourself.

Where money is concerned, refusal to lend is often less offensive than the acrimony that may be caused by attempts to get it back. If you

GENERAL BEHAVIOUR

must lend money to a friend, prepare to lose both it and them. In fact, a cash advance is probably the politest and most effective way of getting rid of someone you don't really like. Debt causes discomfort, and often the debtor will come to hate those from whom he has borrowed. The best revenge on your enemies is to shower them with wealth beyond the dreams of avarice.

On hearing of the desertion of his trusted lieutenant Enobarbus, Mark Antony responds:

" *Go, Eros, send his treasure after, do it,*
Detain no jot, I charge thee: write to him —
I will subscribe — gentle adieus, and greetings;
Say, that I wish he never find more cause
To change a master. O, my fortunes have
Corrupted honest men. "

William Shakespeare, *Antony and Cleopatra*

CAN YOU USE THESE TICKETS?

From time to time a friend may offer you tickets to some event that he is unable to attend himself. If you want the tickets, for pity's sake, offer to pay. Re-reading that sentence, I wonder for a moment if it isn't too obvious to need saying, but then I remember tickets to Glyndebourne and the Men's Final at Wimbledon which I have been compelled at the last minute to pass on to others. In one case I got not a sou. In the other a few weeks into the following April the recipient said to me 'I really must give you something for those tickets'. As I was trying to think of a none-too-pennypinching way to advise her of the printed price of £80, she handed me a fiver.

WHAT DO YOU CALL THAT THING IN YOUR POCKET?

Never refer to money by any diminutive or pet name – it is tasteless and implies that you are so infatuated with it that although you want to talk about it all the time you are too bashful to refer to it directly. The only doubtful case is that of 'shekel', which may be permissible, but only if you are talking about the modern currency of Israel: if you use it as a sobriquet or euphemism for your own money (or, more likely, that of someone else of whom you are envious), you are making a grave error of taste. The following are some of the words that you should strike from your vocabulary.

Bread	*Lolly*	*Shekels*
Dosh	*Mazuma*	*Spondulicks*
Dough	*Moolah*	*The Stuff*
Folding green	*Oxford scholars★*	*Wad*
Gelt	*Rhino*	*Wedge*

★ *rhyming slang for 'dollars'. Although most Cockneys would recognise the term, none would use it, and few have heard it used, not even on EastEnders, let alone in real life.*

CHARGE CARDS

Charge cards have few advantages: they give you no credit. Most people carry them either because they have been provided by their employers or because they wish to impress their acquaintance with their buying power. Those in the latter category are to be pitied because they have neither friends nor financial nous.

INHERITANCE

If someone comes into money or property, it is tactless to congratulate him on his good fortune: the windfall has come from a tree that the beneficiary will probably have cultivated and may also have loved.

GOING DUTCH

A mad convention in which every member of a group pays for his own share of the bill. Going Dutch aggravates the condition it is designed to alleviate – morbid concern about money. This is because it always affects those who do it in one of two ways: either they hold back on what they order, or else scoff as much as possible to get their money's worth. If you must go Dutch, make sure that you divide the total bill by the total number of people. Adding up who had what is intolerable, as you spend more time paying for the food than eating it.

'And I'll keep the left-over 10p because I had one fewer piece of bread.'

THE MEANING OF MEANS

accismus (ak-SIZ-muhs) *n*. Feigning lack of interest in
something while actually desiring it. [Greek *akkismos*
(coyness or affectation)].

It may be unwise to say that you cannot afford something in the hearing
of anyone who earns – or thinks he earns – less than you, because if that
person is of a covetous nature he will assume – as such people do – that
anyone richer than he himself can afford anything. He will therefore
conclude that you are a miser. And anyway: define 'afford' – most purchasing
decisions are volitional, rather than informed by current solvency.

SOCIAL SITUATION

You are in a restaurant; your host asks if you want a digestif. You're
not sure if you should accept: he may be testing you to see if
you're a boozer; he may not have one himself, and you may not
want to drink alone; you may even be worried that he cannot
afford it. What should you do?

*Decline. Then if he orders one for himself it is safe to assume that if he
can afford one he can afford two, so tell him you've changed your mind.
A good host will sense a guest's inhibitions and put the offer in another
way: 'I'm going to have a brandy. Can I interest you in something?'*

PAYING

Pay discreetly and, if possible, not in front of your guests. Do not carry
a wallet with dozens of sections which cascade like a plastic waterfall to
reveal all your credit and charge cards. Do not say to your companion:
'I need to add service: what's ten percent of £200?'

TIPPING

Taxis

In 1995, an article in the London *Evening Standard* newspaper declared that it was 'non-U' not to tip a taxi driver or a hairdresser. That was, and is still, nonsense. Tips should be given only to those people who have provided something over and above the letter of the contract. If you are going to tip as a matter of routine, what will you have left to give when someone renders you a real service? People tip London cabbies because they fear a torrent of abuse if they restrict their payment to the exact amount shown on the clock. This is clearly a very bad motive, and incurs unnecessary expense.

In the late 1970s I took a taxi from Belgrade Airport into the city centre. I would have been hard pressed to name the local language, let alone speak it, and had even less idea about the accepted nuances of Yugoslav behaviour. When we reached the Hotel Moskva I asked the driver if I should tip him, and he replied with dignity in decent English: 'That will not be necessary'. *Autre pays, autre moeurs.*

Although most of the invective that may be heard at the nearside window of a London taxi comes from the mouth of the driver and is directed at the passenger, I know of one role reversal. In the 1990s, a university graduate, having taken a dislike to the milk-round in his final year, came to the British capital and did The Knowledge. On the day he got his badge he took a well-heeled punter home from the West End. On reaching Peckham the passenger glanced at the fare on the meter and paid the exact money. 'Here', said the cabbie, 'What about a tip?' He thought it was the thing to say: he didn't want to be exposed as an Oxonian. 'A tip?' the man replied. 'You want a tip? I'll give you a tip: never wipe your arse with a broken bottle'.

Dustmen

For many years British house-holders were held to ransom by dustmen who knocked on their doors in the latter part of December and wished them a Happy Christmas. Did they care whether you had a Happy

Christmas or rotted in Hell? They did not. They were angling for a tip, some would say they were almost threatening you for it. Whether that was actually their implication or the householder's inference, the fact remains that many people took these seasonal greetings to be a code for 'If you don't want next year's rubbish strewn all over your front path weekly, cough up now'. Men of good will should resist that sort of thing with all the strength at their command: you can be a thief without saying 'This is a stick-up'.

Hairdressers

Hairdressers should not be tipped: you can't go through life tipping people you see regularly and with whom you are uniquely intimate. By tipping them you complicate the psychological dynamics of your relationship. If you tip once, you must always tip, for fear of causing offence. What if on one occasion you don't have enough change?

You will be flustered, and the hairdresser perplexed and insulted by any departure from the tradition you have thoughtlessly established. And what if one haircut is better than another? Do you grade the bonus accordingly? Don't start anything you may not always want – or be able – to keep up. On the other hand, if you've already been tipping for the last half-century, you should either stick to the established practice or change to a different crimper.

In restaurants

In a restaurant, tip the staff if you feel like doing so, but do not tip the proprietor.

According to the editors of *Harden's London Restaurants*, the practice to which regular diners-out object most strongly is that of leaving the credit card slip blank even after service has been added. Such importunacy should be resisted: if the staff try it on, give them nothing.

" Ninotchka: 'Why should you carry other people's bags?'
Porter: 'Well, that's my business, Madame.'
Ninotchka: 'That's no business. That's social injustice.'
Porter: 'That depends on the tip.' "

Ninotchka

IS THIS A STICK-UP?

He was walking through the forest. Coming towards him were three men in bast shoes. He went up to them and said:

'I'm frightened of you, brothers. You are three and I am alone.'

'We'll sit down on the grass', they said, 'so that you shouldn't be afraid.
You can stand a few paces away and we'll talk.'

The three men sat down and asked:

'You wouldn't have a piece of bread? We haven't eaten anything for three days.'

He gave them all the bread he had, and went away.
Later they were caught and shot in town.

Andrey Sinyavsky, *Unguarded Thoughts*

SELF STYLING

Don't call yourself or describe yourself in writing as 'Mr': it's a courtesy title that should be left to others to apply to you. If, shortly after you have been elected to a chair your bank issues you with a chequebook on which it has styled you 'Professor', send it back and get them to change it.

In general, women should be governed by the equivalent rule, although exceptions may be made in cases where they feel it necessary either to emphasise their marital status or to ensure that they are addressed as 'Ms'.

FORMS OF ADDRESS

One of the most basic rules of etiquette is to get other people's names and titles right. Forgetting them altogether may be excusable, if only on grounds of senility, but calling Darren 'Darwin' is invariably insulting. What goes for personal contact applies *a fortiori* to written communication. No matter how much people may tell you they love reading, deep down they are looking for a reason to stop, so a writer who does not wish to have wasted his time must do all he can to keep the reader sweet. In a letter there is no better way of turning honey into vinegar than by getting the name or title of the addressee wrong. If you need to write to an official and you are in doubt about his name and/or full title, first ring his office to check.

ADDRESSING PEOPLE

AMBASSADORS

An ambassador from or to Great Britain is called 'His Excellency' or 'Her Excellency'. An ambassadress is the wife of an ambassador, not a female ambassador. The husband of an ambassador has no style. The ambassador's country should always be mentioned, as in 'His Excellency the Ambassador of France' or 'His Excellency the High Commissioner for Canada'. (High Commissioners are ambassadors to and from Great Britain and the Commonwealth countries.) The adjectival form is usually acceptable, as in 'His Excellency the French Ambassador'. The United States' Ambassador to the Court of St James should be formally addressed as 'The Honorable'; socially however, it is acceptable to address him as 'Your Excellency'.

Formal letters to ambassadors should begin 'Your Excellency', social letters 'My Dear Ambassador' (or 'My Dear High Commissioner'). The formal ending is 'I have the honour to be, with the highest consideration, Your Excellency's obedient servant'. 'His Excellency' precedes all other titles, as in for example 'His Excellency Dr Sir Henry Wooton'.

THE CLERGY

Archbishops

The Archbishops of Canterbury and York are members of the House of Lords and letters should be addressed to 'The Most Reverend and Right Honourable the Lord Archbishop of…'.

Letters to either should begin 'Dear Archbishop' and end 'Yours sincerely'.

In person, the formal address is 'Your Grace', the social form is 'Archbishop'. An archbishop should be referred to in his presence as 'The Archbishop'.

Bishops

In writing they should be addressed 'Dear Bishop', and the letter should end 'Yours sincerely'. The envelope should say 'The Right Reverend the Lord Bishop of…'. He should be called 'Bishop' face to face.

Rectors and Vicars

There is now no real difference between a Rector and a Vicar, although historically a Rector was in receipt of greater tithes than a Vicar. Tithes were abolished in 1936, and Vicars are now appointed to all new livings. They should be addressed as 'The Reverend' – 'Reverend' alone is always wrong. In person, they may be called 'Mr' or 'Father' (depending on which they prefer) or 'The Rector' or 'The Vicar'.

Other Ranks

Most other strata of the clergy may be addressed simply by their titles in writing and in person: hence 'Archdeacon', 'Canon', 'Prebendary', 'Provost'.

DOCTORS

Only doctors of medicine should be addressed as 'Dr'. It is pretentious and a lapse of taste for doctors of anything other than medicine to expect to be so described. The most famous non-medical doctor was Goebbels. Doctors of medicine are properly addressed as 'Dr' unless or until they become surgeons, after which time they are always 'Mr'.

ESQUIRE

In Britain 'Esq' used to be written after the man's name to show that you were writing to a gentleman; to leave it off was a snub. Today, egalitarians affect to despise it, but as a compliment it can do only good. It is also pleasant to be able to imply disapproval by omitting it. You should not address anyone as both Mr and Esq: he is either one or the other. If you don't know the person's forename or initial, you will have to address him as Mr; if you don't know that it's a man to whom you're writing, you will have to use his or her full name, without any courtesy title.

HONOURS

You should include the major honours when writing any but the most intimate and personal letters to those who hold them. Whether you include the minor ones – MBEs, for example – depends on the recipient's preference, which you should try to gauge beforehand. Generally it is regarded as socially unacceptable to draw excessive attention to miniature gongs, and so they tend to be omitted.

Today, economic necessity has dictated that many aristocrats have become middle class, and in acknowledgment of the facts of life they tend to drop their titles at work. The Duke of Wessex, for example, uses Edward Windsor as his *nom de travail*. The children of hereditary peers are generally embarrassed to be addressed as 'The Honourable', and what goes for them should be true of a life peer's children, although they are similarly entitled.

KNIGHTS

Until fairly recently, knighthoods would almost always have been mentioned, but even they are now sometimes omitted. In August 1995, Kirsty Wark, presenter of BBC2's *Newsnight*, repeatedly addressed and referred to the Conservative MP for Burton as Ivan Lawrence even though he was knighted in 1992. Sir Ivan, being a gentleman before he was a knight, did not draw attention to Ms Wark's gaffe. On the other hand, the Chairman of British Telecom pulled up a BBC Radio 4 interviewer who referred to him as 'Sir Iain Vallance' before he was knighted.

In April 2005, Michael Bischard was introduced by John Humphrys on the BBC Radio 4 *Today* programme as 'Lord Bischard'. 'It's not Lord, it's Sir', the knight said immediately.

The order of knighthood has been diminished, if not actually brought into disrepute, partly by the fact that in recent years it has been awarded to many showbiz types whose *métier* is not served by mention of it. Thus David Frost, Elton John and Jimmy Savile are frequently referred to – especially in television credits – without the 'Sir' to which they are all now entitled.

In the case of Sir Elton, some people are annoyed (or affect to be annoyed) that he is not known as Sir Reginald, Reg Dwight being his real name. This is silly, because while everyone has heard of (and heard) Elton John, few have heard of Reg Dwight. Only time will tell if this is the thin end of a wedge, and that soon there will be no name too far-fetched to have a 'Sir' stuck in front of it. Then again, perhaps we will never be entertained by Sir Egbert Nobacon or Sir Fatboy Slim, no matter how much work they do for charity. Unless, of course, Her Majesty decides otherwise: nice customs curtsy to great queens…

PEERS

" One of the hassles in life is that no one understands the difference between a viscount and a lord. "

Viscount Thurso

In the United Kingdom there are five grades of the peerage. These are, in order of precedence: dukes, marquesses, earls, viscounts and barons. There are no barons in Scotland, where the equivalent title is 'Lord of Parliament', usually abbreviated to 'Lord'.

Dukes

Letters to a duke should begin 'My Lord Duke' if they are formal, 'Dear Duke' if social, or 'Dear Duke of Dalston' if you are slightly acquainted. The formal valediction is 'Yours faithfully', even if you know his name; socially, 'Yours sincerely'. The envelope should be addressed either to 'His Grace the Duke of Dalston' (formal) or 'The Duke of Dalston' (informal).

In person, a duke should be formally addressed as 'Your Grace'; socially, he may be called 'Duke'. He should be referred to in his presence as 'the Duke' by all persons other than members of his staff, the latter should refer to him as 'His Grace'.

The wife of a duke should be addressed as 'Madam' or 'Dear Madam' in a formal letter. All other forms of address are as for a duke, in each case substituting 'Duchess' for 'Duke' and 'Her' for 'His'.

The correct forms of addressing the other four echelons of the English peerage are the same as those for a duke.

LORDS

A letter to a Lord should begin: 'My Lord' or 'Dear Lord Newark'. The formal valediction used to be 'I have the honour to be, my Lord, Your Lordship's obedient servant', but today 'Yours sincerely' is ample. The envelope should be formally addressed 'The Rt. Hon. Lord Newark'; socially, 'Lord Newark' will suffice.

On formal occasions, a Lord should be addressed as 'My Lord'; socially, you may call him 'Lord Newark', unless he has invited you to use his first name. As a result of the egalitarian spirit of the age and the increasing number of life peers who may be embarrassed by being bowed and scraped to, it is increasingly common for lords to permit — and in some cases, to insist upon — the use of their forenames. When life peer Lord Tebbit, was interviewed on television by Clive Anderson in 1995, he made a point of saying that everyone still called him 'Norman', and invited Anderson to do likewise. A baronet friend of the author would always pre-empt anyone who was about to introduce him as 'Lord X' by proffering his hand to the stranger and announcing his Christian and surnames. Other lords insist on being addressed formally by title, and it may be that they require it even from their intimates. If in doubt about how to address any member of the peerage, one should err on the side of caution and stick with the title.

A member of the peerage signs himself using surname or title alone: e.g., 'Yours sincerely, Newark'. If someone phones you and tells you that his name is 'Newark', you will naturally assume that he is 'Mr Newark' (see Mr). But if he is in fact Lord Newark, he will not, being a gentleman, so describe himself. This may cause a small amount of embarrassment, but it will all be cleared up easily if correspondence is subsequently entered into.

When you are talking about a Lord in his presence to others, refer to him as 'Lord Newark', do not call him 'His Lordship' unless you are a member of his staff.

THE PUBLIC

Master

A courtesy title given to male children under teen age. It may strictly be applied to any male who has yet to reach his majority, but it might appear patronising if used on a seventeen-year-old. It is currently out of fashion, but for no good reason. If you want to use a courtesy title on a letter to an older boy, use Mr or Esq.

Miss

A courtesy title for women who are unmarried or operating in a professional capacity in which for a number of reasons they may prefer to use their maiden names. It is now widely superseded by the preferable 'Ms'.

Mister

If you ask someone his name, assume if he gives a one word answer that that is his surname. Gentlemen do not call themselves 'Mister', they leave it to others thus to address them.

Ms

There is no reason why a woman should have to make any public declaration of her marital status. Men don't have to. Some people object to 'Ms' on the grounds that it contains no vowel sound, but the benefits that derive from the use of the term more than outweigh this. If you're unsure whether a woman is married or not, using Ms will cause no offence.

'Russell as in Crowe?'
'No, Russell as in Bertrand.'

I have from time to time had occasion to reveal my name to trades people of a certain station – let us call them for want of a better generic term 'estate agents' – and they have proceeded to call me 'Russell'. Not wishing to be transported back to school, I have then been forced to point out the error of their ways. Natural breeding or inhibition (take your pick) has prevented me from saying 'Actually it's Mr Russell', so I say 'Actually it's Henry Russell'. And then they call me Henry, which isn't what I want either.

HONOURING THE DEAD

Use 'Mr' and 'Miss', 'Mrs' or 'Ms' only for people who are alive: the dead have bigger fish than etiquette to fry. This precept should be observed particularly in literary essays: if you refer to 'Mr Chaucer' or 'Miss Austen' you suggest they're still with us; 'Chaucer' and 'Austen' should convey the idea that they're not composing but decomposing. Similarly with honours – if you talk about the work of Sir Terence Rattigan, you should strictly be referring only to those works the dramatist wrote after he was knighted. Now that he's gone to his long home you can avoid tying your prose in knots by just calling him Rattigan. There are customary exceptions to this rule, however: one is the poet Sir Thomas Wyatt, who has retained his title ever since his death in 1542; another is Sir Arthur Sullivan (ob. 1900).

THE QUEEN

To meet the Queen of England is both a great honour and a nerve-racking experience. It should be borne in mind that, like all members of the royal family, the Queen is vastly experienced at dealing with people who do not know how to deal with her, and she is widely thought to be unrivalled at the art of inoffensive conversation with and on almost any subject.

In person

To feel at ease with Her Majesty, it is useful to take note of the following points:

• When you meet the Queen, you bow if you are a man and curtsy if you are a woman. You should bow with the head only, not from the waist. Your jacket should be buttoned up whenever you are standing in Her Majesty's presence. The first time you address her, you should call her 'Your Majesty', and thereafter address her as 'Ma'am' to rhyme with Pam, not with smarm. If you refer to her in her presence you should say 'Her Majesty' or 'The Queen' – for example, do not say to a newly arrived third party: 'She was just talking about that'. If you ask Her Majesty about her family, you should refer to them by their titles – e.g., you should ask if the Prince of Wales has recovered from his broken arm, not 'how's your eldest getting on these days?'

• It used to be the form to prefix any remark made to the Queen in person with the phrase 'May it please Your Majesty'. This is now out of date and should not be used.

Bow with the head, not from the waist.

Correspondence

If you are writing to the Queen, it is usual to write in the first instance to The Private Secretary to Her Majesty The Queen asking him to submit your letter for Her Majesty's consideration (or approval) or to ask if Her Majesty's attention may be directed to….

In the letter itself you should refer to Her Majesty, not she. You should ask the Private Secretary to place your suggestion before or request an opinion from Her Majesty. Don't get carried away: 'Her Majesty suggested that Her Majesty might attend the gala' is too much: 'Her Majesty suggested that she would' etc. is perfectly a acceptable phrase in this particular instance.

If it is necessary to write to the Queen directly, letters should begin:

Madam,
With my humble duty…

Letters to the Queen should end:

I have the honour to be*, Madam,
Your Majesty's most humble and obedient servant.

* or 'remain', if you have written before

The envelope should be addressed to Her Majesty The Queen.

If you're inviting the Queen to something, first write to the Private Secretary and ask if it's okay in principle to do so. Don't send a printed invitation. The Queen and most other leading members of the royal family fill their diaries about six months in advance. If one royal refuses, you can always ask another: they do not take it as a slight.

THE UNITED STATES

In England social precedence is clearly marked out, but in the United States the pecking order is less codified, though strongly adhered to in some circles. At the head of the list comes the incumbent President, followed by the Vice-President, the Speaker of the House of Representatives, the Chief Justice of the United States and any former President. Forms of address are generally more egalitarian than in Britain, and all high-ranking officials tend to be called 'Sir' or 'Ma'am' (to rhyme with 'ham'). Letters to the President should be addressed to 'The President'. The greeting should be 'My Dear Mr President', the valediction 'Respectfully yours' or 'Sincerely yours'. In person, the President should be addressed as 'Mr President' the first time, and then as 'Sir'. Although former presidents retain their title, there is nothing wrong with newspaper journalists and broadcasters referring to 'former President Clinton', because to continue to call him President in almost any context would be misleading. He should still be addressed as Mr President, however.

GENERAL CORRESPONDENCE

CARE OF

On a letter, you are care of ('c/o') a person, but 'at' a place. Thus it should be His Majesty King Duncan at Inverness Castle but c/o Mr and Mrs Macbeth. 'c/o The Sheraton International' is wrong: letters to people staying at hotels should be addressed to 'John Smith, Hotel Guest, The Sheraton' etc. When writing to a hotel guest, it is helpful to indicate his check-in date on the top left hand corner of the envelope: e.g. 'To await arrival 29 February'.

CHRISTMAS CARDS

There are some who maintain that one should ensure that Christmas cards are sent neither too early (in which case it may be thought that one is soliciting a response in order to make one's mantelpiece resemble that of a popular person), nor too late (in case one appears to have only remembered the addressees after receiving their card).

Don't worry – just send your Christmas cards whenever you can, any time in December.

It is a nice touch to write the name of the recipient above the greeting on a card, doing so creates the impression that you have taken some trouble over it.

Non-Christians do not usually worry about receiving Christmas cards – if you are worried about sending them, choose cards with the messages 'Season's Greetings' or 'Happy New Year'.

It is really not good form to write on Christmas cards 'We must meet for lunch, do ring to suggest a convenient date'. You might as well come right out and say 'I'm trying to avoid you'. *(See also Answering machines, page 170.)*

Handing out Christmas cards to all your work colleagues is madness, but so many people do it that there is pressure to conform. Either make a point of not sending any yourself, or else bite the bullet: you will at least have the consolation of not having had to pay postage.

No one will think the less of you if you don't send cards at all – provided, of course, that you keep in touch in some other way.

Contempt for Christmas circulars – impersonal encyclicals in which families give a round-up of what they've done in the previous year – increases as the practice of sending them becomes more commonplace. Yet it is wrong to condemn them all out of hand because, like any prose work, they can be informative and entertaining if only they are well written. So anyone who can write intelligibly, concisely and with minimal self-regard should not be put off by the ignorant prejudice of others. Sadly, however, the world is full of writers who do not write, and non-writers who do little else.

LETTERS

The main problems are the greeting and the valediction. The writer is often unsure whether to address the recipient as 'Dear Mr Smith' or 'Dear John'. Although it is always better to err on the side of caution and stick to 'Dear Mr Smith', you may like to try 'Dear John (may I?)'. Alternatively, when writing to people you've met but do not know, you may try the variant 'Dear John Smith'. Do not address by his forename anyone whom you have never met and with whom you have had no previous dealings. Be respectful, never familiar.

It is not unusual to find that the name of the person you need to contact is sexually indeterminate: Chris Smith could be a man or a woman. If in doubt when writing, use the full name every time: he or she will just have to accept the omission of the usual 'Mr', 'Ms' or 'Esq'. If you're telephoning, ask for Chris Smith and you should be able to get the sex from the voice. You could ring up and ask if Chris Smith is a man or a woman, but that's hard to carry off without embarrassment. It is also not uncommon to find that the name of the person you have been given a note to telephone is unpronounceable. I recently saw a big yellow 'Police Incident' sign that invited witnesses to ring Detective Inspector Dyche. In this case, you would either have to ask the telephonist for the correct pronunciation or hope that you get through on a direct line which the officer answers with the words: 'DI Dyche'.

The general rule about the valediction of a letter is that it's 'Yours faithfully' when it is to someone whose name you do not know and has therefore started with the greeting 'Dear Sir' or 'Dear Madam' or 'Dear Sir or Madam'. A letter to a named person should conclude 'Yours sincerely', unless you know them well enough to use one of the more intimate forms – 'Yours truly', 'Yours ever', 'Best wishes', even 'Love'. Generally, letters addressed to people by rank alone should conclude 'Yours faithfully', even if you know their personal names. There are no longer taboos about typing or word-processing personal letters unless they're of a particularly intimate nature. Putting the 'Dear John' in his own hand is a nice touch used by prime ministers.

THANK YOU CARDS

Unless you know the host well, you should always write a thank you note after anything but the most informal get-together. The exception is children's parties: you took your brood away at the appointed time (*see Punctuality, page 123*), what more can any reasonable parents expect in the way of gratitude?

Some self-styled authorities on etiquette demand that wedding gifts be acknowledged before the ceremony. The practical problems of this are too daunting to contemplate. Have pity and let the newly-weds leave their thank you letters until after the honeymoon.

If you diligently send presents to nephews, nieces, grandchildren or godchildren on their birthdays and at Christmas, remember that in turn, it is a solemn part of their traditional duty to put off thanking you until at least a month has elapsed (and even then only in reaction to chilling threats from their parents). It may be that during the intervening period you start to wonder if your gifts got there at all, but you don't want to ring in case it seems too pushy. Console yourself that if you miss one of the great days in their lives or if the parcel gets lost in the post, they'll be on to you soon enough to see if you're dead.

THE THIRD PERSON

Invitations and replies in the third person ('Sir Rufus and Lady Winckler request the pleasure of your company at...'; 'Peter Schlemiel thanks Sir Rufus and Lady Winckler...') are on the cusp of fashion: many people still write them, but a growing minority regards the practice as too stiff and formal for the present day.

So neither hope nor fear that you will cause a sensation if you reply using 'I' or 'We' to an invitation in the third person. However, in cases of doubt, it is probably better to use the third person, taking as your model Gaius Julius Caesar, a country boy who did well for himself and eventually became a god.

DRESS

For most occasions you know how to dress, you just do.
You either copy the general style of your host or produce
an idiosyncratic variation on the theme. If you've got a
function to attend and you don't know what to wear, don't
reproach yourself – it's the responsibility of the person
extending the invitation to make the dress code clear. If he
hasn't done so, don't hesitate to seek clarification. In the
absence of further and better particulars, wear what you
feel good in. And if you pitch up in smart casual to find the
other guests in morning suits try not to be embarrassed
because it's not your fault.

BLACK TIE

The words 'black tie' on an invitation mean that a man should wear a dinner jacket in black Barathea* with matching belt-less trousers and a black bow tie. The jacket may alternatively be white but the trousers must always be black with a single black braid covering the outer leg seam. The shirt is normally white with a turned-down collar and a plain piqué front, fold-back cuffs and cufflinks. Some men also wear a black waistcoat and/or a black cummerbund. Socks should be black and preferably made of silk. Shoes are usually plain black but may be patent leather as long as they are not on their first outing – if you need to buy a pair, make sure they're broken in before the night of the dinner. Among the possible variants are frilled shirts, wing collars, braided jackets, velvet jackets, fancy waistcoats, coloured cummerbunds and/or 'arty' bow ties.

For women black tie is less clear. Any length of dress can be worn, and even a top and skirt or a trouser evening suit are now widely acceptable, as long as they are smart. Black should be the dominant shade, however.

*Barathea is a worsted fabric with twill hopsack weave; silk or silk-and- worsted fabric with lightly ribbed or pebbled weave.

DECORATIONS

If decorations (medals) are to be worn, the invitation will say so. Do not wear them unless explicitly invited to do so. Do not feel compelled to wear them, however, unless the Queen or another member of the royal family will be in attendance, in which case it might seem churlish not to parade the honour they have bestowed on you.

Holders of several decorations may decide to wear only their highest honour. Since few people other than military dictators wish to appear with all their gongs, it is usual to limit the number of dress medals to four. On a dinner jacket or a dark suit, medals should be attached to the breast pocket. For open-air events such as Remembrance Day marches, medals may be worn on the left breast of an overcoat. Neck badges may also be worn with any of the above garments.

Always give precedence to the honours awarded to you by the head of state of the country you are in. Remember that an embassy counts as a part of the nation it represents, not of the land on which it stands.

DRESS-DOWN FRIDAYS

These seem to work satisfactorily in some companies, but significant numbers of employees (and visitors, too, where they're expected also to observe the local custom) find it excruciatingly difficult to strike a happy balance between the normal sober three-piece and the weekend lycra leotard. If you are a member of staff, imitate the style of your peers without copying any one of them; and if you're an employer who is contemplating the introduction of Dress-down Friday, think again.

FOOTWEAR

Unless they are band-leaders, men should wear black leather shoes with black or grey suits. Brown leather shoes are generally regarded as too casual for business wear, while suede shoes are seen as raffish. Two-tone brown and white shoes are known as co-respondent's shoes because they are thought to have been the footwear that would be worn by the sort of fellow who gets named in another man's divorce. Although co-respondent's shoes are now uncommon, they are no longer entirely disreputable: indeed, Brian Johnson wore them when broadcasting as the cricket co(r)respondent of the BBC.

A woman of breeding and taste will eschew footwear with heels as high as circus stilts. She will also think twice before wearing sling-back shoes with trousers, if only because, although she herself sees no harm in the combination, she is aware that it is deplored in some circles. Some authorities deprecate women wearing patent leather shoes with skirts on the grounds that a man may see the reflection of her underwear on her instep. While researching this book, the author interviewed a dozen men who had spent their adult lives vainly looking for evidence to support this fantastic and wishful nonsense.

HEADWEAR

The old advertising slogan, 'If you want to get ahead, get a hat' no longer means much. In most walks of life and social contexts there is no need to wear a hat unless you want to do so or desire protection against the sun, cold or rain.

Some forms of headwear denote status – crowns, mitres, chefs' hats – but not even monarchs, bishops and cooks wear them all the time, they are mainly ceremonial. Even the British police no longer always wear their traditional helmets. Mosques and orthodox synagogues are among the very few places in which the head must be covered, but paper yarmulkas or keppels are available at the entrances of the latter for those who have nothing else to wear.

In general, men should remove their hats when indoors, particularly in church. When greeting someone, the hat should be doffed or the wearer should at least touch the brim. Hats should always be removed in the presence of royalty.

A hat wearer will traditionally remove his headgear for a passing coffin as a mark of respect, even if he did not know the deceased.

Women often wear hats to weddings, and do not need to remove them in the church or register office, although they may do so if they feel like it. Hats must be worn at Royal Ascot, but they are no longer compulsory at royal garden parties.

HIGHLAND DRESS

Highland dress may be worn instead of the conventional rig at black tie and white tie functions. In those contexts it is a kilt or tartan trousers with a short, silver-buttoned black, or perhaps dark green, jacket with a bow tie. A waistcoat may also be worn; it too should have silver buttons.

The question of whether a non-Scot should wear Highland dress is tricky. The kilt and tartan are important symbols of national and cultural identity, and anyone who wears them should not appear to be doing so frivolously or disrespectfully. A man may reasonably feel that he should not wear tartan unless he has some ancestral reason for doing so. What, then, if a non-Scot is invited to a Highland dress event? He can either decline out of a sense of propriety, or seek further guidance from the host: it may be permissible to pitch up in a normal dinner suit; alternatively, some Scots will not mind seeing the kilt on a foreigner, even if they raise a slightly ironic eyebrow. Daywear Highland dress is a short tweed jacket and an ordinary tie that may be in a variety of colours but should strictly not be tartan, although some people now ignore that stipulation.

Scot or not, you do not have to have a blood tie to a particular clan to wear its tartan. You can dress in the colours of a relative by marriage, or those of your father's army regiment; you can also wear the tartan of a clan that is strongly associated with where you live or somewhere with which you feel a special affinity.

Some books advise that, if you have to wear tartan but there is none to which you're entitled, you should wear the plain Hunting Stewart. However, there is no reason why you should choose that over any other, it just happens to be most commonly stocked by hire shops. Wear the one you like, or what suits you, and be fairly confident that few people are going to cross-question you. If in doubt, kilt suppliers can help.

If you admire a Scottish writer, or even an author of distant Scottish extraction such as Mikhail Lermontov (a corruption of Learmonth), you could wear the tartan of his clan. And if you're asked about it – as you almost certainly won't be – you will have something potentially interesting to talk about.

HORRIBLE HISTORY

Under the Dress Act of 1747 the English banned the wearing of Highland dress in public. The penalty for a first offence was six months' imprisonment; repeat offenders faced seven years' penal exile. The law was repealed in 1783, and thereafter tartan became something of a fashion accessory for the English upper classes, but there is no reason why a civilised 21st-century Sassenach should base his sartorial approach on that of supremacist Regency dandies.

JACKETS

Men should not remove their jackets at formal dinners unless they are specifically given leave to do so by the host. This leave will almost never be forthcoming except on the very hottest day or when the air conditioning breaks down. Men should never ask to remove their jackets.

LOUNGE SUITS

On an invitation this means that you are expected to wear a business suit consisting of a matching jacket and skirt or trousers. The word 'lounge' may raise the hackles of those who have sitting rooms, but it beats 'business', which they no doubt regard as an even more vulgar term.

MONOGRAMS

Monograms are always in bad taste, especially those that appear on shirts and cufflinks. However, if they have been engraved or sewn onto a gift from a loved one, you will probably have to wear them in his company if at no other time because to leave them off might cause offence.

POPPIES

If you're going to wear a poppy, don't put it on before All Saints' Day and take it off at the end of Remembrance Day, the nearest Sunday to 11th November. Only British politicians and television personalities who want to appear patriotic have poppies on from the middle of October.

SHORTS

Some companies – even those that have no particular dress requirements – frown on men in shorts. Although I would not myself be seen dead at work in anything above the ankle – the office may be a jungle but it's not a safari – I have no problem with people who take a different view.

Shorts do, however, tend to arouse adverse comment, and I don't make the rules, I merely report custom and usage and do all in my power to avoid unwanted comments on my legs.

TELEVISION WEAR

Since many people now appear on television – not just as resident presenters or talking heads, but to give of their expertise in interviews or their opinions in vox pops – it is as well for them to have some idea of what to wear on air. The importance of appearance is perhaps even greater on the box than in real life, because if the viewer decides that you look like an ass, you are an ass, no matter how much pith and moment your utterances may contain. And if what you wear distracts the audience from the message, you might as well not have bothered to show up at the studio.

TV DOS AND DON'TS

Do	Don't wear
Make sure your hair is combed	*Black, white or very bright coloured clothing*
Wear plain colours	*Patterns, especially fine, regular ones such as herringbone that strobe on screen*
Accept any professional offer of make-up, especially for studio interviews	*Fussy necklaces*
	Badges
	Tie- or lapel pins
	Dangly earrings

If the audience and fellow guests are too busy looking at you, they won't hear what you have to say.

TIES

In current fashion, a tie of normal length is preferable to a bow tie, if only because it conceals the buttons, which – if not exactly repellent – most people would rather not see. It also helps to hide any postprandial marks on the shirtfront.

BOW TIES

The man who can knot his own bow tie on the rare occasions that he needs to wear one is a more imposing figure than the man who feels the need to wear a bow tie every day.

TIES OF AFFILIATION

Only a cad would wear the tie of a club or society to which he does not belong. If the accused in an English court tries to present himself sartorially in a way that might mislead the jury into thinking he's a better man than he really is – if for example a career handbag snatcher turns up in a regimental tie – and if he refuses to change when asked to do so, the court may be told of his previous convictions, which in normal circumstances go unreported unless and until the accused is found guilty.

" *'What is that tie?' she asked. 'Surely it's not...'*

'No, no', he said, flashing the truth at her so unexpectedly that she was caught a victim to the charm she hated. 'I've promoted myself. It's Harrow.' **"**

Graham Greene, *England Made Me*

TROUSERS

Some companies and restaurants still dislike women wearing trousers. On men, however, they continue to be regarded as obligatory. (*But see also Highland dress, page 53.*)

UNCHANGED

The word now seldom appears on invitations, but if it does, it implies that you should come straight from work wearing whatever you had on there. The underlying assumption is that you are a clerical or managerial type who is either habitually suited or else at least 'smart' in the conventional sense: if you are a gardener it does not mean that you don't need to remove your soiled boots. If you're going on to an 'unchanged' do after a dress-down Friday (*see page 51*) you may care to look at yourself in the mirror before leaving the office. The word should not be used on invitations to weekend events, because on their own time people might wear anything, and a wise host will not wish to open Pandora's wardrobe.

WATCHES

Digital watches which peep on the hour should be avoided unless essential to one's occupation. Those who wear them to the theatre are making the ultimate *faux pas*.

Fob watches are almost stylish, but can look as if they have been dragged into reality from a costume drama. They impress, but they make their wearers appear to be trying too hard. It's as if a fob watch were an alternative to a personality rather than a reflection or extension thereof.

WHITE TIE

Today, 'white tie' seldom appears on wedding invitations. It means that men should wear a black or grey tailcoat, black or grey trousers with double braid down the outer seam, and a stiff-fronted shirt with detachable wing collar fastened with mother-of-pearl or gold studs and cufflinks. Both waistcoat and bow tie are white pliqué. Shoes and socks are as for Black tie. You can add a black silk top hat, white kid gloves, a black cloak and a black silver-topped cane ad lib.

For women, white tie is less specific. In general it is taken to mean the most glamorous affordable ball gown, the showiest and perhaps even most expensive jewellery, and long gloves with bracelets over them. The gloves should only be removed for eating: shake hands (even with the Queen) with them on.

FOOD AND DRINK

If we are completely self-assured, embarrassment will not be a consideration: we will neither feel it nor cause it. Yet confidence may be undermined by the unfamiliar. Like many other animals, we are most vulnerable while feeding – how can we make witty remarks while we're struggling to get the bones out of the mackerel or fretting about the correct use of the implement on the table next to the lobster that looks like something from a museum of medical history?

BREAD

Victorian etiquette seems to have been that bread slices should be exactly one and a half inches thick. Today, bread at mealtimes may come any way you like it; preferably, there will be an unlimited supply, but it should always be available on demand.

The important things to remember are first, that the bread on your side dish should be broken up with the hands, not cut with a knife. Second, that you should put on the spread – be it butter, caviar, pâté or terrine – little by little, in bite-size portions. Do not spread a large sheet of toast in one fell swoop. Do not break bread over or into the soup.

COFFEE

Postprandial coffee may be served either at the dinner table or in the sitting room. Many people are now off 'real' coffee, because they think that caffeine keeps them awake at night, so decaffeinated coffee, tea and/or herbal tisanes should also be on offer.

CUTLERY

The most important purpose of cutlery is to convey food from bowl or plate to mouth; all other strictures about which implement should be used to eat what comestible are affectation. Having said that, there remain several conventions:

Do not eat anything with a spoon that you can equally well eat with a fork. If you are going to mop up gravy, do it with your bread.

Do not eat anything off your knife: there are no exceptions to this rule.

Never use an item from your own place setting as a serving implement.

If the soup bowl has a plate underneath it, the spoon should be placed on the plate rather than in the bowl when you have finished eating.

If an item of cutlery is set on the table before you but you don't need it, don't use it. Start with the outermost implements and work inwards, course by course. When you have finished, put knife and fork together in the middle of the plate in a 'half past six' position. If you drop any cutlery and there are staff waiting at table, don't pick it up, leave them to bring you a replacement. If they are attentive and doing a good job, they should notice at once: if they don't, ask for it, but don't bother to explain why you need it.

If you talk with your hands, put your cutlery on the plate while doing so, ideally in the 'twenty to four position', but practically anywhere other than at 'half past

six', which will lead anyone observing your progress through the meal to the conclusion that you've finished.

While the cutlery for the preliminary and main courses will be laid to the left and right of the crockery, the fork and spoon for the pudding will ordinarily be placed above the 'north pole' of the plate. When eating the pudding, use both the implements provided, or else just the fork, do not use the spoon alone. Why not, you may ask. Don't ask, no one knows – it is probably because that's the way children eat, and the ultimate aim of every sophisticate is to demonstrate that he is not a child.

Chopsticks are usuall provided in Chinese, Japanese, Korean, Thai and Vietnamese restaurants throughout the world. Use them if you like, but do not hesitate to ask for knife, fork and spoon if they are what you prefer. The staff may think you're a hayseed, but their disapproval is part of the reason you chose to go there.

FISH KNIVES

Fish knives have been derided since the mid-1950s. They were originally introduced by the Victorians because steel cutlery was supposed to affect the flavour of the fish and only silver would do. But how do you account for their silly shape? They are best avoided, but if they do appear on the table at a dinner party, they're regrettable rather than a gaffe. If you want to show historical awareness, you might serve fish with two forks (that's how the British royal family still eats it), unless you are afraid that your guests may think you've run out of knives.

DIFFICULT FOODS

Some foods are usually served with special implements to make eating them, if not easier, at least less unsightly and embarrassing. But there are many other tricky foods which you are expected to tackle with nothing more than the usual cutlery. Here are some hints on how to deal with difficult comestibles on social occasions.

Bananas

Everyone knows how a banana should be eaten, but at dinner parties it is expected that you will peel it by hand, slice it with a knife and then eat the pieces with a fork. Why a fork should be used on a dryish banana when oranges (qv) are supposed to be eaten with bare hands is anyone's guess. Debrett's *New Guide to Etiquette & Modern Manners* even suggests making the first incision into the banana skin with a knife, but that's a bit mad unless you are unlucky enough to get one of those rare bendy ones that are about as impenetrable as a bank vault.

Cheese

Don't take all the thin or sharp end (the nose) of the cheese, because that's where most of the taste and goodness are supposed to gather and to do so is looked upon as the height of selfishness. Eat the rind if you like it; if you don't, cut it off and leave it on the side of your plate. Never cut round the rind on the serving plate.

Grapefruit

Grapefruit halves are always cut before they reach the dinner table, except by practical jokers and sadists. There is more to grapefruit than meets the eye.

Grapes

Don't pick a grape or grapes from the serving dish; rather break off a small bunch and eat them with your hands. I have read that in some homes they provide grape scissors, but I have never seen such things, and fear that if I did I might wonder if they had been transferred for the occasion from the bathroom where they were normally used for cutting toenails.

Lemon

Lemon should be squeezed with the fingers unless it is a thin slice in which case it should be squeezed between knife and fork.

Peas

Peas should be eaten from the back of the fork, after having first been pressed onto it by the knife. Although almost everyone I know sometimes eats them using a fork in the same way as they would use a spoon, to do so in 'polite company' invites adverse criticism and is therefore giving hostages to fortune.

Pips

At dinner parties, pips and stones should be spat discreetly into a hand held close up against the lips, then placed on the plate. In the absence of plates, use any available ashtray.

Spaghetti

Hard to eat graciously or delicately, so probably best not served at anything other than the most casual dinner. In Italian theory it should be eaten with the fork alone (using a spoon is not stylish), but in British practice the key objectives are to make as little mess as possible and to avoid sucking it up from the plate.

Trout

Eat the top part of the body, then remove the head as well as the spine before moving onto the lower half.

Whole sole

Eat the top, then remove the spine.

Whitebait

Eat them whole, heads, tails, bones and all.

DUNKING

Is there a person alive who hasn't dunked his biscuit in his tea or coffee? Probably not. Should you do it in polite company? Probably not. Does it 'matter' in etiquette terms if you do? I revert to the previous answer. However, those who wish to create a favourable impression would do well to be mindful of the danger that a biscuit so immersed may disintegrate 'twixt cup and lip. There are few certainties in human life, but one is that the contract is never awarded to the executive with the sodden Garibaldi down his front.

EATING WITH THE FINGERS

Most foods should be eaten with the cutlery that has been carefully chosen by the host and strategically set out around the bowls and plates. A few, however, may be attacked with the bare hands alone or in an as it were pincer movement with one hand and a knife, fork or spoon.

Apple

No matter how we might eat this fruit in normal circumstances, at a dinner party we should cut it into quarters or eighths with a knife, which is then used to remove the remaining pieces of core and the pips. Alternatively, if you want to remove the skin, make an incision near the top of the fruit and work the knife downwards in circles. If you can get all the peel off in one piece, it'll look stylish, always assuming that anyone is watching.

Then cut into pieces as previously described. Either way, eat what's left with the fingers.

Globe artichokes

Each leaf should be pulled off and the white tip then dipped in the sauce provided. Do not eat the ends you've been holding, but pile them at the side of your plate.

Asparagus

Pick up the white end, dip the green end in the butter sauce and make every effort not to get it all over your clothing on the way to your mouth. You may sometimes even see silver-plated asparagus holders; in contrast to fish knives (*see page 64*) you may ridicule them as much as you like, but only on the way home afterwards.

Caviar

May be and sometimes is eaten with the fingers, although it's pretentious to do so. Better to spoon a small quantity onto your plate and then spread it on toast, which is the only accompaniment it needs.

Corn on the cob

Corn on the cob should be held in both hands by its ends, and nibbled as it is rotated. Since this food is almost impossible to eat in a dignified manner, a caring host may think twice about serving it.

Eggs

Gulls' eggs and quails' eggs are served hardboiled. They should be cracked on the side of the plate, peeled, dipped in salt and eaten with the fingers.

Kumquat

Cut the top off and eat in the hand. Don't embarrass yourself

and fellow guests by trying to dissect it with a knife and fork.

Lobster

If you get a cold claw, it is quite in order to pick it up and excavate the deepest and tastiest recesses of the crustacean with the special lobster fork that ought to have been provided.

Mussels

Hold the shell in the fingers and extract the contents with a fork. Pile the empty shells onto another plate. Finally, use a spoon to eat the soup at the bottom of the bowl. If a mussel isn't open, don't open it – just move it onto the out-tray.

Olives

Olives are quite straightforward until you come to the stone. The natural and polite method of disposal is to put your hand over your mouth, pop it into your palm, and then lose it in the bowl which should have been provided.

Oranges

Peel an orange with the fingers, break it into segments with the fingers, remove any pips with the fingers and then eat it with the fingers. Using a knife or a fork at any stage of the operation will make you look as if you are suffering from hyperaesthesia.

Oysters

Squeeze the lemon and sprinkle the red pepper over them, and eat the contents with a fork. Then, if it's not a very formal occasion, you may pick up the shell and drink the juice that is left behind. Traditionally oysters were eaten only when there was an R in the month, but since refrigeration techniques have made most foods available year-round, if they're there, tuck in, and certainly don't say 'but it's June'.

Pear

Eat this in the same way as an apple, using a knife to cut it into quarters and remove the core and the pips. You may, if you wish, remove the skin, but this is a messy undertaking if the fruit is ripe and it is, in the view of many, something of an affront to the food, a bit like pushing lean pork to the side of the plate and eating only the fat.

Prawns

Peel them manually, wash your fingers in the bowl provided, then use a fork to dip the prawns into the mayonnaise on the side of your plate.

Snails

Unless tongs are provided, it is quite acceptable to hold the shell between the forefinger and thumb while excavating the contents with a fork.

FADS AND ALLERGIES

If there is something you cannot or will not eat, you should advise your host in advance, preferably when you accept the invitation. Vegetarians and vegans should not make disapproving remarks about what neighbouring carnivores are eating. And vice versa.

SOCIAL SITUATION

We once had vegetarian guests for whom my wife created one of the finest lentil bakes in the history of gastronomy, in addition to, and separate from, the flesh that she set before the resident meat eaters. As we picked up our knives and forks one of the visitors asseverated: 'I don't know how you can put that muck in your mouths'. Guess what we did.

We just kept smiling and never invited them back.

FINGER BOWLS

Finger bowls are pretentious unless they are brought to the table with mussels, asparagus or artichokes (in which cases they are essential) or some kinds of fruit (possibly, but not necessarily, including oranges). Dip your fingers and wipe them on your napkin, and remember that it's a gesture, not a rite of purification. The water should be tepid. The hostess should avoid putting anything in it – slices of lemon or flower petals, for example – unless she wants her home to be compared with or mistaken for the local tandoori house.

LAYING THE TABLE

The table is laid with a minimum of two wine glasses, one for white and one for red; there may also be a smaller third glass if port and liqueurs are to be served at the end. There is in addition nowadays usually another, larger glass for water.

If you are intending to serve more than one wine of either colour, you could put out a different glass for each vintage, so that the one will not infect the other. But that's more trouble than it's worth: better to stick to a single wine than to make the table look like the Crystal Palace.

You may put bowls on the table and get the guests to serve themselves, bring the plates fully charged to the table, or present the food in some way in between (for example, give them the meat on the plate and let them add their own vegetables).

When serving, you should stand on the guest's left-hand side. Serve the most important lady guest first, and the hostess and host last, but otherwise move clockwise around the table. Guests should not start eating before the hostess unless she says 'Do start'. (Nevertheless it is better for the hostess to start than to say 'Start' because the imperative has matronly or schoolmarmish overtones.) Guests should wait for her cue no matter how hungry they may be and however much they fear that the food may congeal during the intervening period. The rationale is that there may be a grace. Unless there are servants, it is normally the host who serves the wine and carves the meat. Never clear away before everyone has finished eating – what do you think you are, a bad restaurant? Coffee can be poured by either the host or the hostess.

PLACE SETTINGS

Place settings may be arranged as shown in the diagram. Note the position of the glasses above the knife tips. The larger glass is for red wine, the smaller for white. A third glass may also be put out if liqueurs are to be served. The outermost knives and forks should be used first; diners should then work their way inwards. Dessert implements are shown above the plate, but they can alternatively be laid beside it. In this case, they should be placed inside the knives and forks nearest to the plates because they will be used last. Standard dinner service knives should be adequate for cutting any meat that is fit to serve – knives with serrated edges are for restaurants. There is nothing to prevent the host from bringing in more cutlery with each course as it is needed, although it may prove noisy and inconvenient to do so.

LEAVING YOUR FOOD

The Victorians thought it wrong to eat the last mouthful of anything: diners were expected to leave a bit of everything in polite little piles around their plates. No one has satisfactorily explained why. Nowadays, things are ordered differently. English chef John Burton-Race, formerly of L'Ortolan in Shinfield, near Reading, Berkshire scrutinises every plate on its return to his kitchen. 'There's nothing more gratifying', he says, 'than plates sent back spotless. It's the biggest pat on the back'. Burton-Race says he also approves of the French custom of mopping up the plate with bread.

LEAVING THE TABLE

If you need to leave the table during the meal, don't ask like a child and wait for an answer; just say 'Do please excuse me for a moment' and go off to do whatever it is that you need to do. But don't do it unless it's desperate.

MENUS

A good menu will be varied, and each course should be a counterpoint to that which preceded it. A three-course meal should be like a symphony. Is this pretentious? *Pas du tout*. If the *hors d'oeuvre* is stodgy, make the main course light. If you serve soup do not follow it with a casserole, because they are both liquid. Patties should not be followed by pie. If apple sauce is served with the main course, do not serve apple pie for pudding. Melon and fruit salad should not appear on the same menu. Cheese soufflé should not be followed by cheese. Always serve one hot dish, even on a hot day.

THE ORDER OF COURSES
SHOULD BE AS FOLLOWS:

Seafood

Soup or pâté

Sorbet

Fish

Meat or fish plus vegetables or salad

Green salad

Pudding or cheese

Savoury

Cheese or pudding

Fresh fruit and/or nuts

Coffee and chocolates and/or liqueurs

NAPKINS

As soon as you sit down at the table, the napkin ('serviette' means the same but the word is never used by people who regard themselves as well-bred) on the place setting in front of you should be shaken out of whatever shape it has been folded into and placed on your lap. It is generally regarded as bad manners to anchor it to any part of your clothing or to your person. Do not, for example, tuck it into the front of your shirt collar or your belt.

At the end of the meal, leave the napkin rumpled on the table. To fold it may be taken as an insult because it suggests you think it might be used again before it is washed.

Bibs are for people who sit in high-chairs – grown-ups should always place their napkins in their laps.

DOILIES

These small ornamented napkins often laid on or under dishes are today generally regarded as the epitome of bad taste. Avoid using them and, perhaps, even the people who do.

🥥

PLACE CARDS

Place cards at the dinner table should be brief, and omit most honours, decorations and degrees. The main exceptions are 'The Right Hon.' (for Privy Counsellors who are not peers) and the suffixes RN, QC and MP.

SOME PLACE CARD LEGENDS

Person	Name on Card
Elizabeth II	HM The Queen
Prince Philip	HRH The Duke of Edinburgh
Prince Charles	HRH The Prince of Wales
Prince Andrew	HRH The Duke of York
Prince Edward	HRH The Duke of Wessex
Princess Anne	HRH The Princess Royal
Duke	Duke of Dagenham
Eldest son of duke	Lord So-and-so
Younger son of duke	Lord Family name
Marquess	Lord So-and-so
Marchioness	Lady So-and-so
Eldest son of marquis	Lord So-and-so
	(*usually father's second title*)
Earl	Lord So-and-so
Countess	Lady So-and-so
Eldest son of earl	Lord So-and-so
	(*usually father's second title*)
Younger son of earl	Mr Forename Family name
Daughter of earl	Lady Husband's forename and Family name
Viscount	Lord So-and-so
Viscountess	Lady So-and-so
Son of viscount	Mr Forename Family name

Baron	Lord So-and-so
Baron's wife	Lady So-and-so
Baroness	Lady So-and-so
Baroness's husband	Mr Forename Family name
Baronet	Sir Forename Family name
Baronet's wife	Lady Family name
Baronet's widow	Dowager Lady Family name
Life peer	Lord So-and-so
Life peer's wife	Lady So-and-so
Life peeress	Lady So-and-so
Knight	Sir Forename Family name
Knight's wife	Lady Family name
Dame	Dame Forename Family name

PORT, *passing the*

The host pours it for the person on his right, then serves himself and passes the bottle or decanter to the left. It then circulates around the table clockwise, and its steady progress should not be impeded – in other words, don't hog it, and don't think that, just because you don't want any yourself, you have no need to involve yourself in its circulation. Port is best served with cheese – some people insist that you can't have one without the other, but this is needlessly pedantic. Port should not be decanted at the table.

SALT

If you want salt and there is on the table a bowl of it with a small spoon, pour a little onto the side of your dinner plate and then distribute it with your knife. If the condiment is in a sprinkler (the presence of which on the table gives some people the vapours), feel free to shake it over your food. You may, however, wish to bear in mind that some cooks are embarrassed or even insulted by the implication that they did not use enough seasoning in the preparation. Then again, since many people are now concerned about salt as a cause of high blood pressure, the chef may take the view that he'll cook without and let them add it if they want.

SOUP

When eating soup, the last drops should be spooned up by tipping the bowl away from you. Soup should be sipped silently from the side of the spoon – putting the whole spoon into the mouth is generally frowned upon.

However, if you happen to like putting the whole spoon in your mouth, or find it more comfortable to do so, you can cover any embarrassment felt or caused by telling people that you are from Austria, where the practice is regarded as okay. Don't break bread into your soup. Soup may be served in small cups and drunk like tea. This practice has the authority of Raymond Blanc's usage at the Manoir aux Quat' Saisons in Great Milton, Oxfordshire.

MORE, OLIVER?

They do say that guests should not ask for seconds of soup. The tortuous rationale is that such a request might be taken to imply that the diners are trying to fill themselves up with what they already know to be palatable through trepidation at what might be in store. But why can't a request for a further helping be taken as a compliment to the chef? Make of it all what you will. Style gurus seem not to object to the idea of the host offering more soup, so presumably in that case it's all right for the guest to accept.

STACKING PLATES

Strictly you should not stack plates on or in the immediate vicinity of the dining table, but take them out two by two and stack offstage. Yet many hostesses do stack in plain view, and it doesn't matter very much, even to the sensitive. It is also acceptable to collect plates by holding one in the right hand, balancing another on the forearm, and then stacking in two adjacent piles. Although that is more widely practised by waitresses than society hostesses, it is a way to go, and if you can pull it off impressive in its dexterity. The helpful guest should take his lead from the hostess – if she stacks, you stack, if she doesn't, don't.

Offers of help with the clearing up, though courteous, are seldom welcome, so are probably better not made. The host wants you there for your social warmth and sparkling repartee, not for your skill as a stacker of the dishwasher.

SUGAR

In a perfectly polite world, white sugar should be served with tea, brown sugar with coffee. You can get away with white sugar in coffee, but brown sugar should not be seen near tea. It is generally regarded as *de trop* to serve both kinds of sugar even if you're serving both beverages. Do not serve sugar lumps unless your home aspires to the condition of ye olde tea shoppe or you are entertaining horses. It is no longer considered necessary to present sugar with tart fruits such as grapefruit.

SUPPER

Supper is the meal eaten after attendance at the theatre. Any other meal between sunset and sunrise is dinner.

TABLE MANNERS

Do not put your elbows on the table until the food has been cleared, and preferably not then, either. This stricture probably first arose to discourage people from eating sloppily, but it is now just a rule to prevent people from getting comfortable at the table.

DON'T READ AT THE TABLE.

DON'T RISE UNTIL EVERYONE HAS FINISHED EATING.

DON'T LEAN BACK IN SUCH A WAY THAT THE FRONT LEGS OF YOUR CHAIR RISE FROM THE FLOOR.

TEA

Some people are against tea in general, because it is a stimulant and a diuretic and stains the lining of the stomach. Others would have you believe that tea bags are naff, but loose tea is now seldom seen outside huge stainless steel urns in cafés, and most of them now use bags too.

China tea should be accompanied by a small dish containing very thinly sliced lemon. Each cup should have a saucer and a spoon. When tea is served at teatime or in mid-morning ('elevenses'), a small plate should be placed under each cup, which the guest should then remove when cakes or biscuits are offered. All other crockery and implements are over the top – there is no need for slop bowls or sugar tongs.

Those who insist on herbal tea appear not to mind their drinks being served to them with the tea bag still in place *chacun à son goût*. But as a host I wouldn't do it.

MIF

If tea is served, it is widely regarded as classy and impressive to offer a choice of Chinese and Indian. If milk is to be taken, it is conventional to put it in before the tea: this is commonly abbreviated to 'MIF' (Milk In First).

This practice originated in the 18th century when tea (then sometimes pronounced 'tay') was drunk from china cups which were liable to crack if boiling water was poured straight onto them. Although bone china is now seldom used, there is still a good reason for observing the MIF rule: if the tea starts off weak, you can identify its shortcoming straight away, and pour half cups all the way round, returning to the first guest who will get a strong second half to compensate for the puny beginning. If you put the milk in last, you won't know how weak the brew is until it's too late.

DRINK

Wine

This is an area in which it is almost impossible to make any general statement. Among the most common rules are those which state that white wine should be served with white meat and fish, and red wine should accompany dark meat. This will usually save an ignoramus from embarrassment, but it is restrictive and holds good only up to a point. Some of the most striking exceptions are grilled scallops, which may be served with red wine that is light and fresh enough not to overwhelm the flavour of the shellfish; and salted cod, for which a solid red Rioja is more than suitable. The list of pairings is almost endless, but some of the most common combinations are given opposite.

One oft-observed rule is that champagne and rosé go with anything. This is not a universal verity – it would, for example, be a waste of champagne to blast it with spicy food – but it's reliable often enough if you're desperate. While it is important that the wine should complement the food and neither overwhelm it nor be inhibited by it, it is at least as important to ensure that, if more than one wine is served with the meal, none should suffer by comparison with that which preceded it, nor should it overwhelm the grape that follows. Complex foods need simple wines, and vice versa.

When serving wine to guests, don't offer them a choice of drink to accompany their dinner before they know what they're going to eat. You know what they're having, so just bring it on.

Before serving, decant fine red wines and port to separate the liquid from any sediment. Decant port at any time on the day of the dinner, red wine between half an hour and two hours before the guests arrive. Pour it out slowly in a good light so that you can see the dregs at the bottom and prevent them from entering the decanter.

If you're a wine snob, or out to impress, you may wish to decant at the table, thus showing off the labels on your finest vintages. In general, however, it is best not to decant at the table because it requires attention, at least some of which should be devoted to the guests.

RECOMMENDED WINE/FOOD PAIRINGS

Smoked salmon	*Champagne, sparkling wine, Riesling, Sauvignon Blanc*
Grilled fish	*Sauvignon Blanc, Pinot Blanc, Loire Valley whites, Riesling, Champagne*
Pork	*Pinot Noir, red Burgundy, Chianti*
Lamb	*Cabernet, Merlot, red Bordeaux, Barolo, Rioja*
Roast chicken	*Pinot Noir, red Burgundy, Chianti, Spanish reds*
Steak	*Cabernet, Merlot, red Bordeaux, red Rhones*
Salads	*Sauvignon Blanc, Loire Valley whites*

Beer

While wine is the generally accepted accompaniment to food, if you have the confidence to bend the rules there is no reason why you should not serve beer as an alternative to accompany a 'proper' meal. Some brews are certainly good enough to hold their frothy heads up in the company of almost any cuisine – Arran Blonde, for example, goes well with the delicate taste of smoked salmon. Nevertheless, you need either expertise or the hide of a rhino to bring this off, and some people might take it amiss if they are offered only hops and no grapes.

Non-drinkers

Soft drinks, typically still and sparkling water, and possibly orange juice, should always be available. This onus is invariably on the host: it would be odd if a guest turned up bearing a bottle of Evian. You may decide not to serve any alcohol at all. Some guests – particularly those who will have to drive home afterwards – may secretly welcome its absence. Never offer one for the road, or knowingly mix drinks which seem innocuous but are alcoholic. Apart from that, you are dealing with rational adults who should know when they're too parrered to drive home.

IN THE
WORKPLACE

No one in his right mind would work were it not for the money. Anyone who claims to do it out of interest or to keep his mind alert is deluding himself. And if he gets a job he soon reveals himself as unemployable. Unless you have the power to change everything that's wrong about your work, pay and conditions, you will have to keep your own counsel; the only incentive is the fear that, if you don't, you may be 'released into the job market'. Once you reconcile yourself to the indignity of labour, work is little different from other forms of social intercourse. You may wish to appear a go-getter, but getting on with your colleagues is not a sign of weakness.

APPEARANCE

If you turn up to work unshaven or with dishevelled hair or with clothing that makes you look as if you spent the previous night in a shop doorway, your employers may conclude that if you take no care of yourself you will be insufficiently attentive to your job responsibilities. Although there is a flaw in this reasoning – the slob may be such a perfectionist in his work that he has neither time nor headroom for grooming – you should bear in mind that in offices dumb ideas may be more highly valued than truth. Take it from Georges-Louis Leclerc de Buffon, even if you don't believe him, '*le style est l'homme même*'.

BUSINESS CARDS

It would be absurd to suggest that to hand someone your business card is a violation of etiquette; nevertheless, cards are a mixed blessing.

The moment for presenting a business card should be chosen with care. It is a well-established national stereotype that Japanese executives give you a card every time they see you, even if they see you eighteen times during the course of a trade fair. Although there are times when you will need to present your card to a flunkey before you can get to the person you want to see, the card is usually best presented as you take your leave. It is perhaps presumptuous to flash it at the start of the meeting – the recipient may not like the implication that he might have to deal with you again. On the other hand, if he asks for it, be quick on the draw.

Since your business card says something about you – something more than just your name and that of your company and your work address – you should take care over the exact form of words that appears on it. Especially that of your job title. 'Sales Representative' is fine, but 'Area Sales Executive' is grandiloquent and thus an error of taste.

CARDS OF IDENTITY

The only unequivocally good thing that ever came out of calling cards is Norman Douglas's *Looking Back*. In May 1897, Douglas acquired in Merano, Italy, a bronze *brûle-parfum* with a long-legged water-bird flying in relief over its curved belly; the lid was formed of a grotesque dog-like creature biting a snake. For thirty years and more, Douglas used it as a receptacle for calling cards, and when he came to write his memoirs he used them as prompts.

'Had these cards been of value they would have shared the fate of other valuables that were sold during one or the other of the financial cataclysms which have enlivened my earthly sojourn; they would have been thrown away long ago, had they been heavy.'

A card which describes someone as something he is not is disgraceful and if it is used to gain financial credit, it could result in the owner going to prison. So if you must describe yourself as something, keep the description close to the truth. Do not use courtesy titles: never for example, call yourself 'Mr', 'Miss', 'Mrs' or 'Ms'.

Should you put the letters to which you are entitled after your name on your card or anywhere else? A small part of me thinks that if you have earned them, you are entitled to flaunt them. The greater part, however, takes the view that if you have a major honour or a degree from an ancient university, your distinction will shine through without the need for show. By the same token, no one will be impressed by a load of letters that mean nothing, and not even the most cogent explanation will raise his level of awe.

In 1962, Barbara Cartland's *Etiquette Handbook* required a business or calling card to be 'three inches long and one-and-a-half inches deep'. Today, almost anything goes, although anyone who has tried to keep a contact list of other people's business cards would prefer it if they were all still, if not these exact dimensions, at least a consistent size.

HIERARCHY

As we have seen, it's seldom the words themselves that cause offence, it's who says them, and when and how. If you see a co-ordinate leaving the office at four o'clock, you can probably get a smile by saying 'Half day?' But if a manager makes the same crack to a filing clerk it will sound like the kind of shot across the bows that precedes the formal warning. *Noblesse* (if that's what you call it) *oblige*.

In the workplace, if you want to talk to a colleague face to face, go to his desk or office. Do not call him in to see you unless you are trying to make a point about your higher place in the corporate pecking order.

JOB APPLICATIONS

Job applications are a crucial part of etiquette. They are advertisements for the self, and as with all advertisements the reader is just looking for an excuse to stop reading.

> *" Des services! des talents! du mérite! bah!*
> *soyez d'une coterie. "*

François de Salignac de la Mothe-Fénelon, *Télémaque*

CURRICULUM VITAE RULES

DON'T MAKE ANY SPELLING MISTAKES.

DON'T HAVE A STEREOTYPED CV, WHICH YOU BANG OUT TO ANYONE AND EVERYONE YOU THINK MIGHT LIKE TO GIVE YOU A JOB. YOU SHOULD DO A BESPOKE APPLICATION FORM FOR EACH VACANCY YOU CHOOSE TO PURSUE, AND TAILOR IT TO BRING OUT PARTICULAR

QUALITIES WHICH MAY BE APPROPRIATE FOR EMPLOYER A BUT NOT
FOR EMPLOYER B.

IT IS UP TO YOU WHETHER YOU REVEAL YOUR MARITAL STATUS, YOUR
RELIGION AND/OR YOUR ETHNIC ORIGINS. YOU MAY BENEFIT FROM
EQUAL OPPORTUNITIES OR POSITIVE DISCRIMINATION, BUT THEN AGAIN
YOU MIGHT NOT. REMEMBER THAT AU FOND THESE MATTERS ARE NONE
OF ANYONE ELSE'S BUSINESS.

DON'T PUT DOWN YOUR PRIMARY EDUCATION.

DON'T LEAVE BLANK YEARS – ALMOST ANYONE WILL TAKE SUCH A
LACUNA TO MEAN THAT YOU HAVE BEEN IN PRISON.

REFERENCES

Referees should be asked in advance. Some prospective employers take them up before they reply to you, so beware. They shouldn't, because they might drop you in the shit with your present bosses, but they do.

If someone asks you for a reference, the only polite response is 'I'd be delighted'. It is usually a solecism to refuse, and it can be expected that refusal will signal the end of the relationship.

Do not ask anyone to write a reference for you unless you are convinced that he or she knows your qualities and can be relied upon to give you a good write-up. It is often helpful if the referee is a pillar of the community. Justices of the peace and doctors impress potential employers more than estate agents and motor dealers, even if you're applying for jobs in property or garage management.

When it comes to composing a reference, the main rule is: if you can't say anything good, make sure that whatever you do say is couched in terms that will not cause offence. Employers are sometimes bright enough to read between the lines of a testimonial, and omissions can sometimes be very informative. And most importantly don't lie – if you describe as 'honest' someone you suspect of having had his hand in your till and he steals in his next job, which he got partly on your recommendation, you can be in trouble with the law. Just say what you can.

JOB INTERVIEWS

These disgracefully contrived situations maintain the façade of civilisation, but are conducted in the most savage and bloodstained glades of the office jungle. Even though he has just been lowered into a depression full of famished cobras, the interviewee has to be polite and punctiliously observe every one of the important niceties in this book and a couple of thousand unimportant ones beside.

Interviewers, on the other hand, can bare their fangs from the off. Even if they are not overtly hostile, they are likely to form judgements on very little evidence. Thus if the candidate is obese, they are likely to conclude that if he can't control his weight, he will not be able to control his budgets. If he does not dress well, they will presume that he has low self-esteem. This is ridiculous, but it is the way all but the most intelligent and conscientious people think. To make matters worse, throughout the western world, employment is a buyer's market – companies have no incentive to take especial care because there are often thousands more applicants to choose from.

Most of the 'don'ts' for an interviewee are the same as those that apply in polite society. Among other important things to remember are:

1. Never criticise your current employer. You'd probably be well advised not to slag off any of the previous ones, either.

2. Some statistical surveys have suggested that the quieter the candidate, the more likely he is to get the job. Well, yes, maybe, but it would be easy to take this to an absurd extreme, and since what one potential employer regards as dignified reticence may be looked upon by another as truculent silence, such studies are of next to no practical value.

3. It is always possible to respond to impertinent personal questions by taking the offensive and replying along the lines of 'That's for me to know and you to find out'. If they ask you what your father does, you may say 'Thanks but he's already got a job'. Nonetheless, wise-arse responses may cause offence and are therefore a violation of etiquette. They are also likely to ensure that you don't get offered the post, which is, after all, the object of the exercise.

4. As far as possible turn all minuses into pluses. Don't say 'I'm afraid I'm married', but 'My wife also takes a keen interest in your micrometer screw gauges'.

5. You may reasonably feel that you don't need to answer tomfool questions, but it's important to maintain the veneer of unruffled cooperation. Play them all with a dead bat. The answer to 'How do you respond to pressure?' should not be 'My eyes tend to roll uncontrollably, I feel nauseous and sometimes I pass out'; that to 'Do you enjoy working as part of a team?' should not be 'No, I'm a sociopath'.

6. Fluency in languages is widely advertised as a pre-requisite for even some of the most menial jobs, but it is generally a great joke. One man's fluency is another man's timeless stasis. If you suspect that the interviewer is the sort of person who would describe as bilingual any applicant who can say '*L'addition*' or '*Il conto*', suggest that the best way to demonstrate your linguistic accomplishment is to continue the interview in French and/or Italian. Then watch him squirm.

LAUDATOR TEMPORIS ACTI

While it's probably essential at the interview to talk about your professional experience, once you're there don't go on about your previous jobs. Even if you have been plucked by a head-hunter from the biggest name in the industry, that does not mean that all its practices need to be implemented at your new job. With companies as with other forms of suffering there is no hierarchy: one is as bad as another. Their good points, if any, may be described, but we should learn not to tell our new colleagues at Marmite that they ordered things better at Bovril.

NEW RECRUITS

Make newcomers feel at home; help them to get their bearings and to come to grips with the parochial systems that characterise any company. Introduce them to their workmates and line managers.

If you are a senior executive, do not tell new managers as soon as they take up their posts that they are expected to sack some timeserver of whom you happen to have tired or whom you now think you are paying too much. Leave them to make their own judgements. Any manager who does not refuse to comply with such a directive is a worm and should never have been hired.

WORDS OF ADVICE

For Bosses
Your employees are all prostitutes: they only want your money. So don't congratulate them: either put up or shut up. A vote of thanks is, with male nipples, one of the three most useless things in the world.

For Underlings
Don't expect praise: it is only at school that work of a high standard is rewarded the following year by another, more challenging remit. If no one's moaning, you're doing fine.

OFFICE ROMANCE

In most jobs you will be safe for as long as your keep your hands out of the till and off other members of staff. But from time to time colleagues become couples. Any consequent increase in discontent among other members of staff may be attributed to their prudishness or jealousy, but the real cause of bad feeling in such cases is often political – the fear that a new amatory alliance may lead to changes in the *status quo*.

In such instances firms have been known to dispense with the services of one of the lovers; either that or the senior management has made it known that it would like one of them to go. Which is quite wrong, of course. Nevertheless it might be a good idea for the new couple to keep the relationship as quiet as possible, and for at least one of them to start looking elsewhere.

What brings you together may yet keep you apart!

RESIGNATION

No matter how strong the temptation to tell your employer where to stick his job, resist it by any means at your disposal, even, as a last resort by reciting this platitudinous workplace mantra:

"On the way up avoid causing pain
To those you may meet on the way down again."

It's a cliché because it's true – remember that you may one day need a reference from them.

Present your resignation in writing and address it to your immediate superior or head of department, don't go over anyone's head. Use words to the effect of: 'After ten happy years I write to tender my resignation' (it is probably as well to avoid using the word 'offer', you don't want it refused now, do you?). No matter what you really think of the bastard and his chain gang, try if you can to say something like, 'I have enjoyed working as part of your team and will be sad to go'. It is courteous to say where you're going to work next, but you don't have to.

The office hosepipe ban remains in force throughout the notice period.

SEXUAL HARASSMENT

It's a place of toil, not a wet T-shirt competition in Ayia Napa. Don't say or do anything that will make your colleagues afraid to walk past your desk or accompany you in the lift. If you admire their pendulous orbs or their rippling six-packs, keep your aesthetic judgements to yourself.

POST IT NOT

A friend of mine once left a Post-it note on the computer screen of, as he thought, a male colleague, on which he had written the message 'Ring Accounts You Slag'. Imagine his surprise when he later returned to the scene to discover that the intended recipient – a prop-forward type – had changed desks the previous day, and that his place had been taken by a woman of twenty, who was weeping like Niobe. The moral is that if you can't use a word to anyone, you should use it to no one.

TEA-ROUND

If you're making tea or coffee, don't just serve yourself, but offer to make a round for nearby colleagues. That goes regardless of whether you are a newly recruited post-boy or the kind of executive who is taken from meeting to meeting by helicopter. Although there may be difficulties in large open-plan offices with too many people to cater for, your co-workers will probably decline politely but appreciate your courtesy in asking. On the other hand, if you are inundated with affirmative responses, keep an eye on which of the recipients of your generosity reciprocate, and amend your circulation list accordingly.

LANGUAGE
MATTERS

———————— ❧ ————————

Even the most unambiguous statements have more than one meaning. If you merely tell someone the time, you are imparting additional information about or creating an impression of yourself through your accent, tone of voice and choice of words. What goes for speech is also true of written communication. Two people may use the same language to an identical level of proficiency and yet remain mutually incomprehensible because they misunderstand each other's subtexts and nuances. We spend a significant amount of our waking lives trying to avoid the pitfalls of speech – if we remember more of our failures than our successes that may be because the former are more numerous.

The link between correct use of language and good behaviour is complex but strong. The abuse of a term may be every bit as bad as a term of abuse, and every bit as much a violation of etiquette.

AMERICAN ENGLISH AND BRITISH ENGLISH

The difference has often been exaggerated, not least by Oscar Wilde who wrote in *The Canterville Ghost* that 'We [the British] have really everything in common with America nowadays, except, of course, language'. Although some words have sufficiently different meanings to be potential causes of embarrassment, transatlantic cross-fertilisation through travel and the media is so great that there is almost never any serious difficulty. The minor misunderstandings that occur from time to time arouse mirth rather than irritation or inconvenience. Thus an Englishman in the United States will not cause an international incident when he asks to borrow a rubber: his real meaning will probably be understood, if only from the context, even though he means a pencil eraser and not what some Americans call a prophylactic. Americans hearing a Brit say that Lord Smith was his fag at Eton will understand that he does not mean catamite, even though the detailed workings of the school system that Brits call public and Americans call private remain impenetrable to anyone without first-hand experience of them.

My visits to New York have from time to time been troubled by communication breakdowns. A Manhattan barman once acted as if he didn't understand what I meant when I asked for a 'whisky and ice', and only got pouring when I translated the order into a 'scotch on the rocks'.

On another occasion I went into a newspaper kiosk and asked the vendor if he had any English newspapers. He looked like it was the maddest thing he'd ever heard, and slapped his hand on the *New York Times*, the *Washington Post* and the *Herald Tribune*, with each blow saying 'That's English; that's English; that's English.' When I told him I meant papers from London, England, he said: 'Oh, you mean British newspapers, British. We don't got no British newspapers'.

TRANS-ATLANTIC ENGLISH

Some words are problematic because they have different meanings in British English and American English. They include:

Word	American meaning	British meaning
billion	one thousand million	one million million★
bonnet	baby's hat	front of car
bum	tramp, hobo	buttocks
chips	potato crisps	fried potatoes
comforter	bed quilt	one who comforts
cot	camp bed	infant's bed with high sides
craps	dice game	shits (verb)
fag	male homosexual	cigarette
fanny	backside	female pudenda
faucet	water tap	pipe inserted into barrel to draw liquid
fender	wing of car	fireguard to hold in the ashes
hood	front of car	a covering for the head /back of the neck
pacifier	baby's dummy	one who pacifies (almost never used)
pants	trousers	female underwear, gasps for breath
pavement	roadway	sidewalk
pecker	the membrum virile	one who pecks
presently	at once	sometime soon
public school	state school	private school
purse	large handbag	small bag for carrying money
rubber	prophylactic	pencil eraser
trunk	luggage compartment of car	elephant's proboscis or luggage

★ NB The American value of a billion has now been officially adopted in Britain; British texts written before this standardisation took place may therefore be misleading

'But I thought I said you should wear pants!'

The following are some of the words that mean something only in one of the two most dominant forms of English:

• BOBBY PIN, which is what the British call a hairgrip
• the English BOWLER HAT is the same as an AMERICAN DERBY;
• HANDBAG, which has no meaning in the United States
• EIDERDOWN is British English for what Americans call a COMFORTER
• MATHEMATICS, which the English abbreviate to maths, is further shortened by Americans to MATH
• the NAPPY, which is wrapped around a small baby's bottom, is the British word for what Americans call a DIAPER

- PLIMSOLLS (British) are what Americans call SNEAKERS
- RESTROOM means public lavatory to an American but almost nothing to a Brit
- TIC-TAC-TOE is the US term for the game known in Britain as NOUGHTS AND CROSSES
- SOPHOMORE is a second year university student; the British have neither term nor semester for such people;
- only Englishmen wear TROUSERS (cf PANTS).

Although speakers of one language may be tempted to use the other's idioms in order to 'fit in', it is an error of taste to do so.

EXPRESSIONS

Never prefix anything with 'I have to say' because you don't. Let your watchword be the legend on the tablet held by Salvator Rosa (1615–1673) in his self-portrait, *Aut tace aut loquere meliora silentio* (either keep quiet or say something better than silence).

The following expressions should not be used because they are nauseating to the listener and create the impression that the speaker does not give a fig for sensitive language use:

I kid you not	*A whole different ballgame*
Believe you me	*A touch of the old…*
In my judgement	*With [all due] respect*
At the end of the day	*To tell you the truth*
I'll tell you for why	*Quite honestly*
I'm not being funny	*To all intents and purposes*
Period (as in 'I'm just not	*This will amuse you*
doing that, period'.)	*No way, José*

Never begin a speech (or for the matter of that, any utterance) with 'Listen up'. It's the 'up' that's offensive, partly because it's ungrammatical, but mainly because it has the effect of turning into an instruction what should rightly only be a request.

DISREPUTABLE ARGUMENT

In conversation, we should avoid saying anything in such a way that it brooks no contradiction. So don't say 'You can't tell me anything I don't know about that: I've been a teacher/brain surgeon/actress/publisher/ professional jockey for thirty years'.

The fact that you did a thesis on Shelley neither trumps nor invalidates the views held by a recreational reader of the poet's oeuvre; you may have treated more sublimated Electra complexes than I have had hot dinners, but that does not necessarily rule out my explanation of the girl's relationship with her father. Of course it may be that your superior knowledge has given you greater insight, but you have to prove it in the stern heat of light conversation. Don't wave your diplomas around like offensive weapons: they qualify but they do not entitle.

MEANINGS

Those who do not know the difference between 'refute' and 'deny' and 'flaunt' and 'flout' (ninety per cent of Anglophone journalists and politicians) may cause offence to those who do, and should therefore try harder to get it right.

- You can be said to refute a charge only if you prove it to be untrue. Thus a counter-assertion is not a refutation – as is popularly supposed, principally but not exclusively, by the person making it – it is merely a denial.
- The girls may flout the school rules by wearing crop-tops, but in doing so they flaunt their suntans.

Fortunately, language is enormously resilient and recovers quickly from even the worst maltreatment. The abusage of one decade is forgotten and often incomprehensible to the next. In the 1970s, it may be remembered, it was common to find 'situation' added to nouns to make them more sonorous. Hence: tie-break situation; confrontation situation; all situations west; terminating, as Clive James wrote, in 'a pain in the arse situation'. But now, almost no one says this.

'**Hopefully**' was hijacked in the late 1970s and '80s to perform a Germanic function, which should be rendered in English as 'it is to be hoped that'. Thus the famous dictum 'To travel hopefully is a better thing than to arrive' would come to mean 'it is to be hoped that to travel is better than arriving'. Which, it need hardly be added, was not what Robert Louis Stevenson meant when he wrote it.

'**Chauvinist**' is not the right word to describe men who treat women badly and who disapprove of women having equal opportunities. 'Male chauvinist' is no better. The word 'chauvinism' is derived from Nicolas Chauvin, a veteran of the Napoleonic wars who appears in Cogniard's *La Cocarde tricolore* and means only absurd pride in one's country, with a corresponding contempt for other nations. The term that should be used is 'sexism'.

Natives of and things originating in the South American country known variously as '**Argentina**' or 'the Argentine' are 'Argentines' or 'Argentine'. 'Argentinian' is a back formation with an otiose vowel – there is no such place as Argentinia.

'**Begging the question**' is the logical fallacy of *petitio principii* – assuming what is to be proved as part of the proof. For example, we know that everything is for the best because this is the best of all possible worlds. It is not the same as 'inviting' or 'raising' the question.

A '**parameter**' is a mathematical term, which does not mean the same – or anything like the same – as 'perimeter', 'boundary' or 'limit', as it is currently popular to believe.

'**Pristine**' means 'restored to its former state', not 'in mint condition'

An **enormity** is a great crime, it is not 'anything that is difficult'. I say this regardless of cricket commentator Jonathan Agnew, who has referred to 'the enormity of the task facing England' when they need about four hundred runs to avoid an innings defeat.

It is flatulent to describe a period or a time as a **period of time**, except in an unlikely context where it may be confused with menstruation or a full stop. Convicts do not do periods of time.

The germs of other illiteracies are still alive and contagious. A commentator is one who comments: there is no such verb as '**to commentate**'. Almost everyone gets this wrong, even the fine journalist Alan Watkins (charitably, it may have been a subeditor).

Between you and I is illiterate, and its use is offensive to all those who know better.

There are no degrees of **uniqueness**: a person or thing is either unique or not unique: 'very unique' is always wrong. ('Almost unique', on the other hand, is okay.)

GAY

A society that cannot get its terminology sorted is a society ill at ease with itself. The appropriation of the blameless, non-sexual word 'gay' to mean 'homosexual' is regrettable, but not as bad as the subsequent division of homosexuals into 'gays' (male homosexuals) and 'lesbians' (female homosexuals). The only possible reason for this absurdity is that people are under the impression that the 'homo' in 'homosexual' derives from the Latin *homo*, meaning 'man'. Well it doesn't, it comes from the Greek *homos*, meaning 'same'. So 'homosexual' covers both male and female homosexuals and is the *mot juste*. Nevertheless, the kindly will note that anyone who uses the old word today may be taken for a homophobe rather than a lover of language.

GENDER

There is always someone who will write 'Yes please' in the space on the form next to 'Sex'. But 'sex' definitely requires the answer male or female. 'Gender' is correctly a grammatical term: nouns and pronouns have masculine, feminine, neuter or common genders.

Nowadays, however, 'gender' is frequently used instead of 'sex'. The supposed grounds for this are that people only appear to be male or female, and they might perceive themselves as something other.

This may be interesting but it is not convincing. 'We are an equal opportunities employer and we do not discriminate on grounds of race, creed, ethnic background, sex or gender' is flatulent and illiterate.

LAVATORY

Fowler's *Modern English Usage* deprecates the euphemistic use of the word 'lavatory'. Today, men of mould will call this room the WC (short for water closet), the most accurate of the polite terms in use. But for most people, anything goes. Some of the options are polite, others are uncouth. Of the first group, the safest is probably the loo – other possibilities include:

- the geography
- the bathroom
- the little boys' room (though this is twee)
- the restroom

Iconoclasts and rakehells may dare to call it:

- the bog
- the dunnie
- the jakes
- the khazi
- the shithouse

How these go over with the audience depends both on its own predilection and the élan with which they are delivered.

Nevertheless, the most widely accepted term for this place is lavatory. Almost everyone polite who does not call it the lavatory calls it the toilet. Even though it isn't really either (a lavatory being a room in which you wash and a toilet a room in which you dress), lavatory is the one to go for if you feel awkward about the other options. Thrillingly, lavatory is even approved by Nancy Mitford, who describes it as 'U'.

PARTNER

A partner is a business associate. Unfortunately, the term has been stretched by those who are too old or too inhibited, to describe their amatory or sexual companions as 'lovers', 'boyfriends' or 'girlfriends'.

The problem with this use of 'partner' is that it causes embarrassment to those who mistakenly conclude that the barrister of twenty years' call has set up some kind of business with the pneumatic blonde to whom he introduces them at Stringfellow's night club.

'This is my sleeping partner.'

PLURALS

Under the reign of Simon Jenkins, the *Times* issued an encyclical to staff which decreed that they should use the plural after 'anyone' (as in 'If anyone on this paper writes badly, they will be sacked'). This was doubtless inspired by a dim wish to avoid the sexism that some people take to be implicit in following 'anyone' with 'his'. But in English the masculine pronoun may also be common gender. It is absurd to say 'somebody's going to get their head kicked in tonight' and no one in his right mind should say it even if, for the time being at least, it is the form favoured by the world and their (sic) wife. And you can nearly always get out of any such bind by making the whole sentence plural: 'People might get hurt'.

SOME TRICKY PLURALS

'**Media**' and '**criteria**' are the plurals of, respectively 'medium' and 'criterion'.

'**Politics**' is singular, and so is '**economics**'.

The plural of '**stadium**' is 'stadia', but after all the talk of the new stadiums that will be built in London for the 2012 Olympics I fear I've given up on this, at least until after the closing ceremony.

'**Police**' is strictly singular, but only the most strict grammarian would insist on 'The police is investigating'.

'**Government**' is trickier: on the basis of usage you could make a case for singular or plural: choose which you prefer, stick to it, and be confident that neither version will make you seem illiterate as long as it's applied consistently.

POLITICAL CORRECTNESS

Political correctness (PC) strives to avoid implied elitism, colonialism, racism and sexism in the use of language. Thus those who were once known as Red Indians are now to be called 'Native Americans' or 'First Nation'. Previously animate chairmen have undergone a no doubt undesired metamorphosis into 'chairs'; the physically handicapped are sometimes described as 'the differently abled'.

This is largely well-intentioned nonsense codified by bores (the differently interesting). For more than a decade, dust-carts in London had at front and rear the legend 'Operatives at work'. (The old style 'Men at work' was held to discriminate against women.) Whoever thought up the new phrase had some relationship with the English language, albeit a tense and difficult one. He or she was informed or sensitive enough to realise that 'workers at work' was a pleonasm; despite being debilitated by that knowledge, he or she played well the meagre hand that he or she had been dealt and came up with a comprehensible but repugnant compromise solution.

No matter what linguistic egalitarians may groundlessly assert, it is still perfectly permissible to talk about 'Man' when you mean 'all men and women (mankind)', and you can still use masculine pronouns as common gender, as in 'everyone has his faults'. Indeed, you'd be verging on illiterate not to. But if you insist on maintaining these standards, you must be prepared to justify them and to defend yourself against attacks by people who will describe you as 'reactionary' or 'unreconstructed'. (Sticks and stones....)

Compare:

" To boldly go where no man has gone before.

Star Trek (1964)

To boldly go where no one has gone before. "

Star Trek: the Next Generation (1987)

He: 'Who is that rude man?'
She: 'The host.'
He: 'Ugh! What does he do?'
She: 'Write books on etiquette.'

A MIXED MARRIAGE

Working the room at one of my own parties, I came upon a
married couple, whom I knew, but only by their first names.
They were stuck with each other and talking about football.
I gathered that the husband supported Arsenal and the wife
Tottenham Hotspur. 'A mixed marriage', I ventured lightly, and
as soon as I said it I felt the room go cold. Humourless people,
I decided. Suddenly seeing someone on the distant patio whose
glass might have needed charging, I slid away. On recounting
this incident later to my wife she told me that he was a
Rosenbloom, she an O'Shaughnessy.

PRONUNCIATION

" It is impossible for an Englishman to open his mouth without making some other Englishman despise him. "

George Bernard Shaw, *Preface to Pygmalion*

Pronunciation says more about you than a credit card ever can:

Decade, which should be pronounced 'deck-aid', not as in the past tense of the verb 'decay'.

Harass is 'harrus' rather than 'ha-rass'.

The word **Junta**, in which the j should be sounded. '*Hoon-tah*', the pseudo-Spanish pronunciation used by British prime minister Margaret Thatcher to refer to the government of Argentina during the 1982 Falklands War, and since adopted by everyone else who knows no better, is just embarrassing.

Medicine should have three syllables (med-i-sin), not two (med-sin).

Pejorative should be stressed on the first syllable and pronounced 'pee-jer-ativ'. It should never be 'p-jorativ'.

Schedule should be 'shed-yule' if you speak British English but 'sked-yule' if you're American.

These are shifting sands – you wouldn't have believed that it was possible to mispronounce junta until it happened; now you're amazed to hear anyone get it right. How can so many people pronounce nuclear as if it were spelt 'nucular'? You can't blame President George W. Bush for that, although at the time of writing he is the highest-profile offender – it was current before he came to prominence.

AFFECTATION

Still it's better to say all words wrongly than to sound affected. Some of the most prominent Britons have suffered the ill-effects of elocution coaching. Margaret Thatcher (*see opposite*) and her predecessor as Conservative leader, Edward Heath, both came from lower middle class backgrounds and learned to speak 'nobbily' at Oxford University. Or rather half learned, as their vowel sounds always betrayed their origins. (Not that there's anything wrong with making good – you've just got to make sure that, having done it, you speak naturally in a way that's sometimes described as 'staying true to one's roots'.) England football manager Alf Ramsey was an East London boy who, again, almost learned to speak like a toff, but let himself down through some of his locutions, including famously, 'I said I don't want no peas'.

PROPER NAMES

English proper names, especially place names, are notoriously difficult to get right. There's no point in telling you that Leicester is pronounced Lester – only a foreigner would not know that – but some personal names are tricky, too: mispronouncing them can cause embarrassment and perpetrators are sometimes ridiculed for their mistakes. The following is a list of some of the most commonly encountered:

ALTHORP may be Awl-trup

AMPTHILL is Amt-hill

ANSTRUTHER may be An-ster

AUCHINLECK may be Affleck

AVOCH is Auck

BAGEHOT is Baj-jut

BARUGT is Barf

BEAUCHAMP is Beecham

BEAULIEU is Bew-ly

BEDEL may be Beedle

BELVOIR is Beever

BERKELEY is Barclay

BETHUNE may be Beeton

BOUGHEY is Bowy

BRIDSON is Bride-son

BROUGH is Bruff

BROUGHAM is Broom

BUCCLEUCH is Bucloo

CADOGAN is Ka-duggan

CAILLARD is Ky-ar

CAIUS is Keys when it is the
name of a Cambridge college
(see Universities), but Kai-yus
when it is a forename

CASSILIS is Kas-sels

CHIENE is Sheen

CHOLMELEY and Cholmondeley
are both Chumley

CIRENCESTER, the name of a
town in Gloucestershire, may
be Siss-iter or Sis-sister to
the affected, but should be
pronounced as it is spelt

CLAVERHOUSE is Clay-vers

CLERY is Clary

CLOGHER is Clore

COCKBURN is Co'burn

COLCLOUGH may be Coke-ly

COLQUHOUN is Kerhoon

CONGRESBURY is Cooms-bry

CORCORAN is Cork-ran

COWPER may be Cooper

DALZIEL is Dee-el

DE CRESPIGNY is De Krep-ny

DE LA PASTURE is De Lap-pature

DEVEREUX may be Deverooks
or Deveroh

DILLWYN is Dillon

DU QUESNE is Dew-cane

EGERTON is Ej-erton

EYAM is Eem

FARQUHAR is Farker

FARQUHARSON is Farkerson

FEATHERSTONEHAUGH is
Festonner or Fanshaw or
Festinghay or
as spelt. (The popular six-man
dance company of that name
is pronounced The Fanshaws.)

FENWICK is Fennick

FFOULKES is Fooks or Fokes

FOLJAMBE is Fool-jam

FOULIS is Fowls

GEOGHEGAN is Gay-gun

GILDEA is Gildy or Gilday

GILKES is Jilks

GLAMIS is Glahms

GREIG is Greg, unless you mean
the Norwegian composer
Edvard, in which case it's
Greeg

HARDRES is Hards

HARENC is Har-on

HAREWOOD is usually Har-wood

HAWARDEN is Hay-warden
or Harden

HERVEY is Harvy

HOUGH is Huff

HOUGHTON is Howton or
Horton

JERVAULX is Jervis

JERVIS is Jarvis

JERVOIS is Jarvis

KEIGHLEY is Keethley

KEIGHTLY is Keetly

KIRCUDBRIGHT is Kercoobree

KNOLLYS is Noles

KNOWLES is Noles

KOUGH is Keeoh

LASCELLES is Lassels

LAUGHTON is Lawton

LAYARD is Laird

LEGARD is Lej-jard

LEINSTER is Lenster

LEISTON is Lay-son

LEITRIM is Leet-rim

LE QUEUX is Le Kew

LEVEN is Leeven

LEVESON GOWER is Looson Gore

LISTOWEL is Lis-tol

LOUGHBOROUGH is Luff-bru

LYMPNE is Lim

MAGDALEN COLLEGE (Oxford) and Magdalene College (Cambridge) are both maudlin

MACGRATH is Ma-grah

MAGHERAMORNE is Mar-ramorn

MAINWARING is Mannering

MARISCHAL is Marshal

MARJORIBANKS is Marchbanks

MAUGHAM is Mawm

MAUGHAN is Mawn

MAUGHER is Marr

MEAGHER is May-er or Marr

MELHUISH is Mellish

MENZIES may be Ming-iz or Meng-iz or as spelt

MEOPHAM is Mep-pam

MEREWORTH is Merri-worth

MEYRICK is Merrick

MICHELHAM is Mich-lam

MILNES is Mills

MILNGAVIE is Mull-guy

MONZIE is Munnee

MORAY is Murry

PECHELL is peechel

PEPYS is Peeps

PETRE is pee-ter

PETRIE is pee-tree

PONTEFRACT (the Earl of) is Pomfret

POWELL may be pole or as spelt

RUTHVEN is Rivven

ST JOHN is Sin-jun

SAWBRIDGEWORTH is usually as spelt but may be Sap-sed

SCRYMGEOUR is Scrim-jer

SYNGE is Sing

THYNNE is Thin

VILLIERS is Villers

WAUGH is usually Wor but may be Woff

WEMYSS is Weems

WIVENHOE is a short 'i'; it's not W-Ivanhoe

WODEHOUSE is Woodhouse

WRIOTHESLEY is Ry-othsly or Roxley

YEATMAN is Yateman

YEATS is Yates

N.B [1] *It is better to make mistakes than to be seen struggling to avoid them.*

N.B. [2] *Normally the arbiters of correct British English pronunciation, the BBC is not always right. Its preferred spoken form of Doncaster has a long 'a' and rhymes with 'disaster'. That is wrong for two reasons: the people of Yorkshire, in which the town is situated, use short 'a's, and would be quick to point out to effete Southerners that there is no 'r' in 'bath'; etymologically, the name comes from the Latin* castra, *meaning 'camp', which also has a short 'a'. Moreover, the BBC itself does not apply analogous pronunciations to 'Lancaster' or 'Tadcaster'.*

PERSONAL NAMES

Only a fool would use one particular name to represent a type of which he disapproves. If you say 'He's a real Kevin', you can bet that will be the name of the person to whom you are speaking's father.

SOCIAL SITUATION

At lunch with a business contact from whom I thought advancement might befall, he happened to mention that he had a son named Linus. 'Aha,' I said, quickly grasping the opportunity to show expertise and establish a greater rapport, 'you named him after Linus Pauling, American chemist, double Nobel laureate and champion of Vitamin C as a prophylactic against all forms of cancer.'

'No', he replied. 'We named him after the character in the Snoopy cartoons'.

SWEARING

You can now get away with almost anything coarse or scatological in almost any company, except, of course, that of known puritans such as senior members of one's own family. 'Fuck', if not yet commonplace, is widespread in the street, in the drawing room and in the broadcast media. The previously obscene word 'wanker' has been heard on peak-time national radio when children were listening; indeed, it is now sometimes used as a term of affection. On 29 September 2005 one of the presenters of the Today programme on BBC Radio 4 used the word 'bollocks', not in exasperation, but while misquoting someone who had in fact said 'Nonsense'.

'Arse' was almost unthinkable in polite British usage until the late 20th century. It snuck into port under false colours, sometimes disguised as the American 'ass' and at others as toffspeak: you could call someone a 'silly ass' but say it with a long a. That arse has finally lost the bad smell traditionally associated with it is attested by the 21st-century film advert for the Renault Laguna – a car with a distinctively odd-shaped hatch back. The soundtrack features the Groove Armada song with the lyric 'I see you baby, Shakin' that ass'.

The word 'bum', formerly regarded as unutterable in polite company in Britain has come in so far from the cold that waistband pouches are now marketed under the name 'bum bags'. This would have been unthinkable fifty years ago. Even though the noun still means 'backside' it has become acceptable through American English, in which it is a perfectly polite word for a tramp or a hobo.

Until at least the late 1960s 'crap' was taboo in Britain, but it has now moved from the lavatory into the drawing room. It was helped along the hall by, paradoxically, censors, who did not ban radio stations from playing Frank Sinatra's version of 'The Lady Is A Tramp', a song from Richard Rogers' and Lorenz Hart's 1927 musical *A Connecticut Yankee*. The lyric focused British attention on the previously knowable but arcane fact that in American English it is the name of a dice game. Henceforth any naughty schoolboy could bring that usage to his defence when having uttered the word he was accused of swearing, and thus crap got sanitised.

SALES PITCH?

In late 2005 I asked a respectable-looking woman the way to the nearest branch of a well-known chain store. She told me (in a strong Welsh accent), but added: 'Don't go there, though, it's a shit shop'. I may have looked surprised; she then said: 'Sorry, I mean it's a crap shop'.

The word that you still can't say is the so-called 'c-word', which is cunt: this remains unacceptable, and is offensive in almost any context, whether spoken or written.

Despite a general relaxation in attitudes to swearing, many people are still more impressed by a man who is master of polite and non-euphemistic vocabulary than by one who speaks as if he has given his days and nights to studying the locution of the fishwife.

The problem with foul-mouthed speech today is that it tends to put the swearer in the wrong, or at least to weaken his case. If someone bumps into you and you respond with 'Watch where you're [insert expletive of choice] going', your assailant may choose to take offence at your bad language. So through the injudicious use of a single word in the heat of the moment you have renounced what the pious call the high moral ground, and ended up in what insurers call a knock-for-knock situation.

JOKES

In all forms of social intercourse, from chatting at a drinks' party to speech-making on a formal occasion, remember that it is perfectly possible to be amusing without being risqué. This is not a puritanical blast against blue jokes, merely a reminder that there are prudes and puritans everywhere, and it is better not to cause offence. It is advisable always to err on the side of caution.

The most self-assured – or, perhaps, the most careless – can get away with almost anything. This is partly a matter of tone and timing. It is sometimes even possible to get away with blue jokes and other forms of tastelessness by emphasising that you are quoting someone else – this isn't my sense of humour, you understand, but I am fascinated by the mentality of those who do regard it as amusing. Chaucer got away with that approach, but it is potentially hostile terrain, to be entered at your peril.

FOUND IN TRANSLATION

The following extract from Geoffrey Grigson's *Notes from an Odd Country* concerns a French country priest. The quotations are not given in English, and it is easy to see why: while in France they are only slightly off-colour, rather than blue, north of the Channel they are blasphemous and obscene

" *Joseph, his new factotum, had the duty of waking him up every morning at eight o'clock and telling him the weather. Knock, knock on M. le Curé's door.*

'Bonjour, M. le Curé, il est huit heures et il fait beau'…

'Merci, Joseph, Dieu et moi le savons.'

The formula of announcement and answer did not vary a great deal. A week went by. Joseph (and the curé) overslept. Joseph knocked on the bedroom door three hours late, at eleven o'clock. Before he could mention time or weather, the voice came from inside, unvarying,

'Merci, Joseph, Dieu et moi nous le savons: il est huit heures, et il fait beau'.

To which a now exasperated Joseph replied:

'Dieu et vous sont deux vieux cons, il est onze heures, et il tombe de l'eau comme vache qui pisse.' "

MEETING PEOPLE

Meeting kings, queens, presidents, clergy, the famous, the poor, the dull and even the worthless. This chapter attempts to show you how to act when you encounter them at social events, while retaining both your virtue and the common touch; it even suggests a few possible topics of conversation that might engage the most taciturn and self-regarding. Try not to be put off by another person's froideur – remember that once you've broken the ice you can gambol in the cold water underneath.

BOWING

Bowing should be done to royalty only, and even with royalty it is no longer *de rigueur*. Thus a cat may look at a king and even the staunchest republican can hold his head up in the Queen's presence without running the risk of having it cut off the following morning. If you do bow, bow with the head only – do not bow from the waist (*see also pages 41–42*).

Note: members of the royal family leave their own parties first; you should never leave before them.

INTRODUCTIONS

The polite way to make introductions is to present the 'lesser' person to the 'greater'. The younger should be introduced to the older, the man to the woman, the commoner to the peer of the realm, and the *nebech* to the VIP:

'Richard, this is Tommy Tucker; Tommy, Richard Branson'

or

'Have you met Tommy Tucker? Richard Branson'.

THE ARISTOCRACY

When introducing a titled aristocrat whom you know by his first name, don't say 'Ronald, this is Peter Schlemiel; Peter, this is the Marquis of Haringey'. If you do make this mistake, expect to be embarrassed – you deserve to be when your posh friend tells Peter to call him Ron.

If you are introducing someone to Her Majesty the Queen, the correct form is 'Ma'am, may I present Tommy Tucker?' Do not say to Tucker 'Have you met the Queen?' or anything similar, because Tucker is supposed to know who she is. Do not be embarrassed that you have not named Her Majesty.

COUPLES

When introducing couples who are not married to each other, it is usually better not to draw attention to the fact that they are a unit. If their relationship emerges naturally during the course of the conversation, fine, but a good host will avoid implying that anyone is merely someone else's appendage. Indeed, the same courtesy may be extended to married couples, Jane may be delighted to be introduced as 'John's wife', but if there is the slightest possibility that she may feel inhibited or demeaned by being thus put into context, make her plain 'Jane'.

What goes for heterosexual couples applies *a fortiori* to homosexuals: you should never 'out' people in a social setting. If they want their orientation to be publicised, they will bruit it themselves.

FAMILY

If you are introducing your own parents to a newcomer, you should use the names by which you would yourself address them (mum, mother, father, dad or whatever). Thus you leave it to your parents to invite their new acquaintance to call them by their forenames if they so wish. If they do not extend such an invitation, it should be clear to the newcomer that they wish to be addressed by their titles and surnames until further notice. The same rule applies to grandparents; with aunts and uncles, you may use your discretion. Some children introduce their olds thus: 'My Dad, Winston', 'My Mum, Shania'. That's good etiquette as long as it's previously been cleared – tacitly or explicitly – with the fossils themselves.

FAMOUS PEOPLE

Do not gloss the famous person's introduction, do not, for example, say 'Richard Branson, Chairman of the Virgin group of companies'. A good wine needs no bush. If I were to introduce you to Tenzin Gyatso, neither you nor he would want me to add 'aka the Dalai Lama, the exiled spiritual leader of Tibet'.

There's no need to endure a dark night of the soul about any of this, agonising over whether a High Court judge is more important than a Bishop, or a bank robber worthy of greater respect from his fellow men than a convicted perjurer. All you have to do is make sure that they get to hear each other's names. Once you've done that you have played your part, and can duck out and circulate.

If you are not one of those who can carry anything off, you will probably feel more at ease if you do not launch straight in on the subject for which the famous person is best known. It is often the case that 'I really admire your work' can come out sounding more embarrassing than 'I think you can't write/paint/play golf/whatever for toffee'.

AN EASY ESCAPE ROUTE

Fortify yourself with the thought that the famous are probably every bit as nervous about you as you are about them. When novelist Kingsley Amis met people for the first time, he would sometimes invite them to his club, The Travellers'. He would arrange that during lunch a friend would appear and ask him, 'Has the Mozart record arrived?' If the reply was 'No', the friend would know that Kingsley was enjoying his new acquaintance and leave them to it. However, if Kingsley was bored he would answer 'Yes' and immediately adjourn to go and get it, leaving the unwelcome guest to find his own way off the premises.

Author's note: this sly trick was first made public by Anthony Powell in his Journals 1982-86. I can confirm it from personal experience: when I lunched with Amis a fellow indeed pitched up and asked that self-same question. By then, the writer had been talking to me about himself for some time and appeared annoyed by the interruption. He rather snapped at him, I felt, saying no, it had not arrived. 'I think you'll find it has, you know, Sir Kingsley', I protested.

The American actor and comedian Emo Philips was accosted by a stranger who asked him rudely: 'Have I seen you on television?' To which he replied: 'I'm afraid I don't know: unfortunately you can't see through the other way'.

'I REMEMBER YOU'

What do you do if the person to whom you have just been introduced says that of you but you have no recollection of him? This hasn't happened to me often, but when it has I seldom feel that I've got my response completely right. I tend to squint myopically and say 'Aaah, yes, of course' in a way that I imagine comes across as faintly suspicious. So although I do not prescribe that approach, I think it's preferable to a flat contradiction – if he's right, and you've simply forgotten him, or if you're right and he's confusing you with a mass murderer, there will be embarrassment. The best tip is to the person who purports to do the recognising: say where you previously met, but make sure it wasn't somewhere like a brothel.

*'Do you know Mark?' asked the host.
'Of course I do!' replied Henry.*

LATECOMERS

When you have to introduce tiresome late arrivals long after all the other guests have been presented to each other, cut corners in order to avoid disrupting the conversation which it is to be hoped will by now be in full flow. Say their names once to the assembly, and then tell them the names of the first couple of people who meet them close up.

PROFESSIONALS

The trickiest commoners you can meet at a social gathering. Do not ask barristers 'How can you defend someone if you know he's guilty?' and do not expect free on-the-spot medical advice from doctors. Both professions would almost rather be asked how much they earn.

TITLES

Guests with several titles can be introduced with only their main one, or the one of which they're most proud, or that which explains the capacity in which they're at the do. Thus the ambassador 'His Excellency Dr Sir Henry Wooton' may have some of his titles omitted in the interests of brevity and of not overawing other guests. However, if you know that His Excellency likes to hear them all, or suspect that he might, make sure he gets them.

If you have forgotten the names or titles of your guests yourself, you have a choice. You can either brazen it out by saying 'You all know each other', or you can be honest and say 'I must apologise, I've had a complete mental blank'. The latter takes guts, and it is better not to attempt it unless you are sure you can carry it off. Remember that etiquette is only breached if offence is caused.

IT COULD BE VERSE

At a party in 1946, Mervyn Horder found himself next to Lord Wavell, then Viceroy of India. By the former's account, they would both, if given the chance, have passed the whole of their lives in unbroken silence. But conversation was the order of the day, and since none was forthcoming, Horder recited the first two lines of a poem by Hilaire Belloc, whose work he knew Wavell admired. At the end of line two, Wavell took over and completed the verse; they did the last line in unison and after that there was no holding them back.

PUNCTUALITY

" L'exactitude est la politesse des rois. "

(Punctuality is the politeness of kings)

Louis XVIII (*attributed*)

Hosts at restaurants should always arrive before their guests. Cocktail and drinks' parties do not go on for long, so try to make it within fifteen to thirty minutes of the stated starting time. It is permissible to be up to an hour late for evening parties at which there is no meal; if it's dinner, you should arrive about ten minutes after the time the host has suggested. If the invitation is from a member of the royal family, or if a member of the royal family will be present, you should arrive on the dot. Children should be taken to and collected from children's parties punctually – plus or minus five minutes at most.

At a routine rendezvous, my rule is this: if I'm not supposed to be insulted if they're ten minutes late arriving, I assume they won't be insulted if I push off after waiting for eleven minutes.

SHAKING HANDS

Most people shake hands with each other when they meet for the first time. Some people shake hands every time they meet, even if they encounter each other every day. Such people are usually – but not always – foreigners. Everyone must decide whether or not he approves of this, and acquiesce or resist as directed by his conscience.

Grasp the proffered hand normally and firmly: do not attempt to make the moment memorable by breaking a couple of its proximal phalanges. Even more important, do not hold the grip and the gaze of the recipient until it causes embarrassment. You don't need to take your glove off for a handshake, but it adds a stylish flourish if you do. Men should always stand to shake hands; women may remain seated even if the other person is standing.

KISSING HELLO

Difficulties may arise over greetings and leave-takings. The British, for example, tend to confine themselves to one kiss on the cheek; mainland Europeans and Britons who have been influenced by them often insist on both cheeks. If you get it wrong – in other words, if you go for a different number of kisses from that which the other person is expecting to give and receive – you will embarrass yourself.

Almost everyone finds air kissing annoying, but nearly everyone does it. So how should we deal with it? We could take the prescriptive, *écrasez l'infame* approach and point out to offenders the error of their ways. But what would be the point? Do you really want the sensation of their lips against your cheeks so badly that you're prepared to ask them for it? Are you prepared to say that you find their refusal to put their mouths on your body offensive?

Sometimes turning the other cheek is the right thing to do.

PUBLIC PUCKERING

Traditions evolve by which you will kiss some of your acquaintances every time you see them and leave others unosculated. So what do you do when you meet someone you habitually kiss in the company of someone else you know and do not? There is no easy answer to this, save the advice that you should either kiss all your friends every time you meet them like some drugged-up theatrical or popular lady novelist, or none of them under any circumstances. The spirit of the age would appear to dictate that those who do not kiss everything that moves are somehow repressed and fuddy-duddy, but it is as well to remember the use to which a kiss was put in the Garden of Gethsemane. Anyway, some people think that kissing is too good to be wasted by putting on a public performance.

BETWEEN THE SEXES

◄

This chapter is based on the premise that copulation is not the only thing implied by 'sexual intercourse'. The term is taken to include all dealings between man and woman that are informed — or more likely inhibited — by the one's consciousness of the other's pudenda. Since most of us spend the whole of our earthly sojourn confined in a single sex, and few of us have the imagination of Tolstoy, there is plenty of scope for misunderstanding and conflict. Numerous barriers remain between people of different sexes even if they are not, haven't been and will never be a couple.

If you need to be told that it is wrong to thrust yourself upon an unwilling partner, or to make invidious pre- or post-match comparisons with previous conquests, you probably need counselling rather than a book of this type.

ADULTERY

"Do not adultery commit;
Advantage rarely comes of it."

A.H. Clough, *The Latest Decalogue*

Adultery is generally frowned upon, although some people like it, and some people have spouses who like them to like it. Unless you are a clergyman or a politician of the right, it is a mistake to condemn someone's adultery out of hand before you know all the circumstances. It is not done to confess or prate to a third party of one's own infidelity. To do so is even worse than boasting of premarital sexual conquests, and a deal riskier.

AN ALIEN PRACTICE

It is noteworthy that in English, adultery is often regarded as something that foreigners do:

"What men call gallantry, and gods adultery,
Is much more common where the weather's sultry."
George Gordon Byron, Lord Byron, *The Corsair*

And the nationality that most often takes the rap is the French:

"Fidelity means nothing, but to stand before God
after death and confess you have never cheated on your
wife — what a humiliation!"
Jules Renard

SOCIAL SITUATION

A man once told me about a time he had been unfaithful to his wife. This is not in itself an unusual occurrence – people often feel an irresistible need to boast of their conquests. I have wondered why, but never identified a satisfactory explanation – all I can think is that they want to impress the audience. Two particular details made this confidence, which I need hardly add I had not solicited, especially distasteful. The minor one was circumstantial: he gave it a sordid local habitation – a hotel in Brussels while on a business trip. The major one was that he seemed to have forgotten that I knew him only through his poor wife, who had been my friend for 15 years, and who introduced him at a painful 'meet my new significant other' evening shortly before they became engaged. Plainly this is a dilemma, how should one resolve it?

I can only tell you what I did not do. I did not warn him that he should not be telling me such a thing, because of course by this time I realised what he was saying he had already said it. I did not look disgusted, and I did not affect awe. I made like the Sphinx. Moreover, I did not tell the betrayed woman. So instead of answering the question, I merely put another: who is demeaned by this? Not the coxcomb who publicised his Belgian swordsmanship; nor yet the wife, who as far as I am aware knows nothing of it to this day: no, the only net loss was sustained by the poor wight who had to hear the confession and then felt obliged to keep it to himself. I wish now that I'd gone the whole hog on the Sphinx front and hurled the ghastly traveller to his death on some nearby rocks.

ASKING SOMEONE OUT

The only consolation that can be offered to young people who suffer from embarrassment is that they will not always feel it. Sooner or later it withers and falls away, as the snake sloughs its skin. But in the meantime asking someone out on a date is one of the most frightening social leaps that a youth can make. The trick is to frame the invitation in such a way that both parties are left with an honourable path of retreat. Tell the invitee that you're going out with a bunch of mates, and ask her if she would care to join you. That way she gets the idea that you are interested, but has neither to say that she finds you the antidote to desire nor to enter a contract for life.

*'Is this seat taken?' may not work if there is only one chair and the
person addressed is sitting in it.*

An invitation to dinner à deux may or may not be seen as a sexual overture, it depends on the circumstances. It's okay if the proposed venue is a restaurant – it's a public place and the exits are not barred, so both parties have a means of escape if need be. It may even be okay at home. There is no need to take the mystery out of the underlying purpose, if any, of the date – don't say anything along the lines of 'on the understanding that it's purely platonic' or 'I want you to know there's more to this than just dinner'. Neither party should assume too much. Hope is more fun than certainty, but uncertainty creates fear: the middle way is narrow, but it is not un-navigable.

NO ONE WANTS TO HEAR HOW HAPPY YOU ARE

It may be that you want or need to repel someone's advances because you are already taken with or by another. If that's the case, you don't necessarily need to tell the suitor point-blank that you are married or content in a long term sexual relationship: find a way of dropping it into the conversation in a plausible context. And a word to the suitor: take note of the information thus imparted and consider yourself warned off; be grateful that you have suffered no loss of face; don't say 'Are you getting enough?'

SOME OTHER TIME

This no longer means anything other than 'Not in a million years'. So if you really can't make the suggested date, but would like to go out with the person who's asking, you must either suggest a specific alternative ('The 19th's out, I'm afraid, what about the 23rd?') or make it clear in another way, perhaps by saying: 'I can't make the Mozart, but there's a season of Vivaldi coming up in June that I'd really like to go to. Would you be interested in that?' If that goes over well, either of you can get the tickets: there's no longer any reason why it should only be the man.

ARE YOU NOW OR HAVE YOU EVER BEEN...?

Asking people point-blank or making speculative assertions about their sexual orientation ('I always thought you were gay') may cause offence. And doing so takes out one of the best parts of life: gradual discovery.

JEALOUSY

It is an error of taste to display jealousy. If your partner is making advances to someone else in your presence, leave him to make a fool of himself: moral superiority and *sang froid* give you an unbeatable hand. If you assert yourself or get cross, you will lose – you are demeaned by engaging in the farce. Never give anyone the satisfaction of knowing he has annoyed you, and remember that if he is going to run away with the person with whom he is cavorting, he'll do it whether you defend your territory or not. Above all, there is no less aesthetically appealing sight in social life than that of two people rucking about fidelity.

OLD FLAMES

What if you used to have a secret or long-forgotten liaison with someone who is, was or has since become famous? Should you tell others – your intimates or anyone who will listen – of the big one that got away? Circumstances alter cases, but in general it is better to keep these conquests or submissions quiet. Apart from being ungallant, such talk smacks of desperation, sounding as if you need to prove your (former) desirability or man-of-the-worldliness. Moreover, it is like Graham Greene's claim that he played solitary Russian roulette: impressive if true, but unverifiable.

STANDING

Men who are seated should stand when a woman enters or re-enters the room at a formal or even slightly smart occasion. It is sometimes necessary to use one's judgment over this and avoid bobbing up and down ludicrously as she comes in and out of the room. There is usually no need to do it if there are numerous guests and the female arrival is at the far end of the table. If you are in mid-course, just carry on eating unless it is a particularly formal occasion, in which case a small bob in which the buttocks are lifted a couple of inches from the seat of the chair will suffice: there is no need to go for full elevation.

On trains and buses, seats should be given up only in cases of need. It is no longer the done thing for a man to offer a woman his seat if there are no others available simply because she is a woman. If the woman is pregnant, carrying a small child or in any kind of apparent difficulty, a seat should be offered. It is perfectly in order for a woman to offer her seat to a man, but again this should be done only in case of need and should not be interpreted by the man as a come-on.

SEXUALLY TRANSMITTED DISEASES

Sex is too big a cheese to be served up with small potatoes such as etiquette. The method of contraception, for example, is not a nicety, a subject you might raise to cover a lull in conversation – it may be a matter of life and death.

Sexually transmitted diseases (STDs) of all kinds are on the increase. In Britain and the United States today, 20–25% of people have had at least one affliction of this type before the age of 20. If abstinence proves unworkable, how should we conduct ourselves?

Manners' guru Moyra Bremner advised people to ask each other just before they go to bed together for the first time if they have any STDs. This idea is as affecting in its simplicity as it is preposterous as a realistic course of action. Does no one lie about these things? Did no one ever forget one or two small inconvenient details about himself when the blood was hot? And if it turns out that one participant has a full house of venereal conditions,

to what extent is the other partner indemnified by earlier assurances to the contrary? None whatsoever.

Of course, if you ask the question and get an affirmative answer, or better still, if your prospective lover confesses in advance without prompting, at least you know where you stand. (The problem of precisely when to ask or when to announce the bad news remains tricky – over the coffee or under the duvet?) But if you ask the question and you get a no, you will still have to use your judgement.

Both the hunter and the quarry should probably always carry condoms and as many good luck charms as they can decently have about their person without appearing too superstitious. The former accoutrements should, however, be kept under cover: it is presumptuous, and hence an error of taste, to have them on semi-show at the top of an open handbag or sticking out of the back pocket.

WALKING WITH WOMEN

According to medieval tradition, when a man walked with a woman he was supposed to position himself on her right-hand side, so that his sword arm was free and also presumably so that he didn't bang her with his scabbard. While it is highly likely that even in Plantagenet times not every man wore a sword, today still fewer are so armed in public; nevertheless, the custom survives, although it may be preferable for the man to position himself so that he is closer than his female companion to passing road traffic. Again neither party should make a song and dance about this: the woman should neither insist on such treatment nor protest if she doesn't receive it; the man may try to ensure that that's his position, but he should not draw attention to the fact that he is doing it.

ESCALATORS

Even in an age of women's liberation and equality of opportunity, it is still the done thing for the man to go ahead of the woman on an escalator. This is to ensure, in the event of an emergency stop, the woman's fall may be cushioned by the man (the male of the species is still usually acknowledged as physically stronger than the female). On an up escalator, it is also to prevent the man looking up the woman's skirt. You may think the latter reason absurd, but it's still better to stick to the rules. On the other hand, there is equally no point in making a big deal of it: just try to get yourself into whichever position it behoves you to be in, but if the other person presents trenchant opposition, let commonsense prevail. The purpose of such a courtesy is to ease the running of society; it is not an end in itself. Your obituary will mention your Fellowship of the Royal Society, your parents, school, university, wife and children, usually in that order: it will almost certainly pay no tribute to the manner in which you conducted yourself between the second and third floors of Harrods.

RITES OF PASSAGE

There are three events at which everyone wants to fit in – they are sometimes referred to colloquially as hatches, matches and despatches. Birth celebrations and baptisms are quite low-key affairs. Weddings have bacchanalian aspects, but guests who proposition the bride or shout out a just cause or impediment why the happy couple should not be joined are largely the stuff of fiction and nightmares. At funerals even the most unorthodox and flamboyant should forego their normally constant quest for attention in deference to the feelings of the bereaved.

BIRTHS

The first news of the birth of a child is normally conveyed by the father, who rings relatives and close friends within a few hours of the arrival. The nearest and dearest will want to come and visit, but they should first find out from the father if mother and baby are well and strong enough to bear it. If and when the well-wishers do come, they should reckon to stay only for about twenty minutes or half an hour.

Presents for the infant may be almost anything – from a teddy bear to a fixed-term investment fund that will mature on his 18th birthday. You've got more or less carte blanche for the mother, too: cosmetics, unguents and anything that will help her to feel feminine after her ordeal are often welcome. So too, usually, are flowers (*see also page 160*) – if they are sent to the hospital, rather than brought in person, check first to see if the mother is registered in her maiden or her married name.

Any elder siblings may feel usurped by the new baby and resentful of what appears to be their parents' lack of concentration on the children they already have. Recognising that, some friends and relatives give presents to the ones who fear they've been forgotten.

MAKING THE ANNOUNCEMENT

If, in addition to informing people by word of mouth, the parents decide to make an announcement in a newspaper, the form of words need be no more than a bald statement of the fact:

PRIMLEY – *On 1 June, to Jacob and Lucy, a son.*

(There is no need to put the year: that will be at the top of the page, nor do you yet need to have decided on a name.)

Nevertheless such notices are widely accompanied by further information which, though strictly otiose, adds to the occasion:

PRIMLEY – *On 1 June, to Jacob and Lucy, a son, Jason, a brother for Hector and Lucretia.*

They may even stick in an epithet – 'beautiful', 'miraculous' – after the first indefinite article. Some people object to that practice, but there is no harm in it. Other details, such as 'a long-hoped-for grandchild for Ron' may have purists muttering disapproval, but it's not their gig – if it sounds good to you, play it.

Some parents announce the birth by mailing cards. That's a good thing, but many would advise them against incorporating a photograph of the mother before she's had a chance to freshen up or of the child before he has been cleaned up. On stiffened paper no larger than a postcard (14 x 9 cm), and possibly even as small as a business card (*see page 84*), the legend should be along the lines of:

Jacob and Lucy Primley are happy [or proud, notwithstanding that pride's a deadly sin] *to announce the birth of a son, Jason, on 1 June 2006.*

To that may be added, to taste, the place of birth and the child's weight.

CHRISTENING PARTIES

There is no standard form for christening parties, but they tend to be fairly small and select occasions at which champagne is normally served. There should also be a christening cake, which usually resembles a baby-size wedding cake. If there is to be a proper meal it is traditional to ask the clergyman who performed the baptism to say the grace. There is often a toast to the baby, and this may be proposed by one of the godparents.

Guests at christening parties are expected to take presents for the child. They should wear suits or similar smart apparel.

GODPARENTS

Children usually but not invariably have three godparents – two of the same sex, and one of the opposite sex. This tradition is based on Church of England practice, in the Roman Catholic church, it is conventionally one godparent of each sex. The father's best man is often one of the godfathers to the first male child

Godparents receive no guidelines other than those set out on a small handbill given to them at the church on the day of the baptism. They have no legal rights, but the role carries spiritual and financial obligations. The godparent is supposed to be available any time the child may need advice or guidance. This is largely moonshine, few godparents will ever want or be in a position to knuckle in on the parents' domain.

It is an honour to be asked to be a godparent, and it is almost impossible to refuse such an invitation. It is scarcely even acceptable to decline on religious grounds, because religion no longer has very much to do with it. If you really do not want to be a godparent, the only inoffensive excuse is to say that you have so many godchildren already that you fear you will not be able to give another the attention he deserves. Failing that, you really have no other course than to accept graciously and ensure you make a good job of it.

In theory, the function of godparents is to guide the godchild from baptism to confirmation. Thus the best-qualified godparents should be familiar with the Bible and are probably themselves active Christians. In practice, however, most parents ask their closest friends to be godparents, partly to compliment and honour them, and partly to secure for their children an unfailing supply of Christmas and birthday presents. The godparents' own religion seems no longer to matter, and many churches do not even inquire about appointees' beliefs. However, some clergymen still hope to see evidence of a vague predisposition on the godparents' part towards the teachings of Christ, even if it is now too much to expect them to be full life and afterlife members of the church.

Presents

Presents for godchildren are seldom easy to choose. The first gift is given on the day of the baptism, and is usually an item of silverware – napkin rings, apostle spoons, forks and those absurd food pushers of which there is no recorded use in human history. Some people lay down wine or port, which will mature at about the same time as the child will first be legally permitted to drink it, but others object to this practice on the grounds that alcohol is an enemy of promise and something the child can be relied upon to discover for himself. If you want to give wine or port, ask the parents first and be prepared to take no for an answer.

For the first four or five birthdays and Christmases you can ask the parents to identify an appropriate gift; thereafter you can get the child to tell you himself.

CONFIRMATION

Godparents are expected to attend the child's confirmation service, which, if it takes place at all, will usually happen when the child is in his early teens. Here again a gift is expected, and don't jump to the conclusion that a copy of the Bible will do: he will almost certainly have acquired one of those as soon as he started preparing to receive his first full communion.

Strictly the godparent's duties end when the child is confirmed. Although some adults continue sending cards and presents on the godchild's birthday and at Christmas for the rest of their lives, many take the first full communion as their cue to stop; a few carry on until the child reaches the age of majority, before they, too, decide that the ritual has run its course. While it is all right to do that, it is important to let the child know your intention in advance: it is a rare teenager who does not take everything personally, and if his godparents suddenly and unaccountably change their giving habits after more than a decade, he might well think that it is because of something he has said or done.

Even if you come to dislike your godchild or if one of you moves to the other side of the world you must still remember his birthday and Christmas and do everything in your power to take an active, intelligent interest in his development and welfare. If you fall out with the parents, keep faith with the child. Remember that visiting the sins of the fathers upon the children is God's job, not yours.

SHOWERS

Showers are parties that originated in the United States, and are usually held to welcome new arrivals to the community but sometimes to celebrate forthcoming marriages. The setting can be mid-morning coffee, lunch, tea, dinner or a full-blown evening bash. Invitations can be formal or informal, written or telephoned. The idea of a shower is that guests bring presents, which can be used in some specified area. Thus to a bedroom shower, everyone would be expected to bring sheets, pillowcases, towels and the like; to a kitchen shower, cutlery, crockery and glasses. Most showers involve only family and close friends – those from whom a gift would in any case be expected. Presents given at a shower held in advance of a forthcoming marriage are usually in addition to, rather than instead of, a proper wedding present. Those held in honour of a new baby are sometimes called stork showers, and guests are expected to present layettes or toys.

ENGAGEMENTS

When a man and a woman decide to marry, they may wish to announce the fact to interested parties. There are several ways of doing this, the most conventional of which is by taking a notice in the 'Forthcoming Marriages' column of a newspaper. Whether it is a national or a local newspaper depends on whether everyone you wish to inform takes the paper in which you have chosen to advertise. In Britain, the main national for these announcements is the *Times*, but many people now prefer the *Daily Telegraph*, the *Independent* or the *Guardian*. People whose circle of friends and relatives is confined within a small and tightly-knit community may prefer their local rag.

MAKING THE ANNOUNCEMENT

The usual form of words in a newspaper entry is this:

'The engagement is announced between Alistair, son of Mr and Mrs Octavian Losasso, of Tewksbury, Gloucestershire, and Agnes, daughter of Mr and Mrs Barnaby Truslove, of Moreton-in-Marsh, Worcestershire'.

The *Times* will only allow advertisements phrased this way, unless there is to be no engagement as such, in which case the wording 'The marriage will take place…' is acceptable. 'Son' and 'daughter' may be qualified with 'only', 'elder', 'eldest', 'younger', 'youngest' or even, in the case of large families, a number ('the seventh son of…').

The only variants are in the case of death ('daughter of the late Mr Barnaby Truslove and of Mrs Annabel Truslove'); divorce ('daughter of Mr Barnaby Truslove and of Mrs Annabel Truslove'); and remarriage ('daughter of Mr Barnaby Truslove and of Mrs William Collins'). If a parent's change of surname gives rise to ambiguity about his or her relationship to the betrothed, then the child's surname should also be stated.

The other ways of announcing an engagement are by throwing a party or by word of mouth. Both ensure reaching more of the right people (that is, those you want to tell), but neither has the stylishness (to say nothing of the cachet or the snob appeal) of a newspaper advertisement. These methods are not mutually exclusive and none is obligatory – you can always marry one day and announce the fact to your family and friends the next.

An engagement party (as distinct from a party at which an engagement is announced) is usually for only a few relatives and intimate friends, and is not infrequently the occasion of the first meeting of the bride's parents and the groom's. The only point of etiquette at an engagement party is that the bride's father may propose a toast to the couple, and the groom may reply, thanking all those present for their good wishes and proposing a toast to both sets of parents.

The announcement of an engagement is usually organised and paid for by the bride's family.

WEDDINGS

BEST MAN

The best man is the bridegroom's helper at the wedding. He is there to lend assistance and be a combination of Johnson's Boswell, Wooster's Jeeves and Crusoe's Man Friday. Indeed, British Royal bridegrooms tend to call their best men 'supporters', a term that describes perfectly the role of the best man.

It used to be held that the best man should himself be unmarried, but this rather pointless custom has now fallen into disuse and may safely be ignored.

The groom may, if he wishes, have two best men, as did film actor Peter Sellers when he married Britt Ekland and singer Elvis Presley when he married Priscilla Beaulieu.

There is nothing to prevent a woman from being a best man. The most likely objector is of course the bride, but American divorcée Fanny Osbourne had no known misgivings when her groom, Robert Louis Stevenson, chose his friend Dora Williams to support him at their wedding in San Francisco on 19th May 1880. Stevenson later described Williams as 'my guardian angel and our best man rolled into one'.

The most onerous part of the best man's role is the speech in which he replies on the bridesmaids' behalf to the toast proposed immediately beforehand by the groom. Among the best man's other main duties are:

1) To organise and accompany the groom on his stag night. He should ensure that the Groom gets as drunk as he wants to, and gets home in one piece.

2) To carry the wedding ring on the groom's behalf and make sure it does not get lost. A good best man will probably carry a cheap, spare ring as a stand-in in case the worst happens and the real ring falls down a churchyard drain.

3) To read out telegrams from those who were invited but unable to attend. These usually contain straightforward messages such as 'With all good wishes on your great day', but may also attempt to recycle well-worn jokes: 'To the bride from the groom's Football Club, 'We've tried him in every position, now it's your turn'. A good best man will decide on the spot whether or not such gems are fit for the assembly.

4) To hand the presents from the bride and groom to the bridesmaids during the course of his speech. (This is not invariable, some newly-weds give the bridesmaids the presents themselves after the Reception.)

BRIDEGROOM

He appoints the best man and the Ushers (*see page 150*), he pays for the wedding ring and all expenses incurred at the place where the marriage itself takes place. He should also arrange and pay for the bride's and bridesmaids' bouquets, the buttonholes of his own attendants and any further flora that may be required around the place. He should also sort out the going-away transport and the honeymoon. But the above is all on the assumption that he or his parents can afford it, the financial burden can be spread around if necessary without embarrassment.

BRIDESMAIDS AND PAGES

The bride's attendants before, during and after the wedding ceremony are appointed by the bride and tend to be her brothers and sisters, nephews and nieces or closest friends. If one of the women is herself married, she is known as a matron-of-honour. The bride should give them each a present either privately, after the wedding, or during the reception. If during the reception, it is usually handed over by the best man (*see pages 144–145*) during his speech.

CONGRATULATIONS

At an engagement party or a wedding reception, you should congratulate the groom on his choice of bride. That is, you should say 'Congratulations'. It used to be thought unacceptable to congratulate the bride on her choice of groom, because of the overtone of entrapment it was thought to convey. Fortunately this is one of the areas from which equal opportunities have effectively swept the cobwebs of cant. The only rule is: gush! Gush regardless of what you really think of the tart or gigolo in question.

PRESENTS

If you have accepted an invitation to a wedding you must either take a present or arrange to have one sent. Presents are usually sent to the home of the bride's parents.

Many couples compile a wedding list, which they will send out on request. (Some people send it out, unsolicited, with the invitation, but that is bad form.) There are two kinds of wedding list. Sometimes the couple will go to a department store that offers the service known as 'The Bride's Book'. There, with the help of an assistant, they compile a list of the goods they need/hope to receive. They then advise guests of the shop in which the Bride's Book is held. The guests telephone, visit the shop, or look on its website, make their choice and pay the bill. The item is crossed off the list and sent to the home of the Bride's parents. This avoids duplication of gifts.

A NO-FRILLS APPROACH

Compare the practice at a Greek Cypriot wedding. There, no presents are expected, but during the service members of the groom's family pass among the congregation and offer buttonholes to the male guests. Anyone who takes a flower becomes the groom's *koumbaros* (which loosely translates as something between 'best man' and 'sponsor'), of which there can be any number. The *koumbari* then participate in the protracted Greek Orthodox ceremonial exchange of rings. Later, at the reception, they are picked out by the family and they must then use a pin to stick money onto the groom's clothing as he dances with the bride. This is a refreshingly candid approach to what is at heart a business transaction: a wedding is really no different from a bottle party, and there are names for people who turn up at those without any wine.

The second method is to circulate a wedding list with no particular shop in mind. The guests should then tell the Bride which item they propose to buy. She will then delete it from the list herself, and the guests will be left to make the purchase from a shop of their own choice.

Another method is to have no list at all, and leave the choice entirely to the guests. Couples who adopt this course often object to a conventional wedding list on the grounds either that 'we'd prefer them to buy us something personal, without any prompting', or that 'it seems too much like overt soliciting'.

To the first objection, the answer is that without a list you run the risk of returning from the honeymoon to a dozen pop-up toasters. To the second, the answer is more complicated. It is implicit in a wedding invitation that a party is being held at considerable expense in the expectation of a return on the investment in the form of presents. The British are reticent perhaps to a fault about these financial realities.

In North Dakota, USA, some couples raise money by holding an auction at the reception in which the highest bidder is permitted to remove and keep the bride's garter.

If you decline an invitation to a wedding, it is up to you whether to send a present. You may send a telegram – if you do, bear in mind that, by tradition, it will be read out by the best man during his speech at the reception (*see pages 144–145*).

REGISTER OFFICE

A Register Office is where civil marriages take place in front of a Registrar and a Superintendent Registrar and at least two witnesses. The bride and groom have to say aloud the following:

'I do solemnly declare that I know not of any lawful impediment why I, (Name), should not be joined together in marriage to (Name)';

and later:

'I call upon these persons here present to witness that I,
(Name), do take thee, (Name), for my lawful wedded
wife/husband'.

The register is then signed by the bride and groom, two witnesses and
the two Registrars in front of the assembly.

Note: It is incorrect to call such a place a 'registry office'.

SOCIAL SITUATION

When English model Jordan married Australian pop singer Peter
André in 2005, they were faced with at least one dilemma. Their
friends Kerry Katona and Brian McFadden had been husband
and wife but were by then estranged. Should they invite them
both separately, just the one they preferred, or neither of them?

In any breakup there is a division of spoils. Friends of the couple may
want to stick with the one they preferred, or the one they think has been
wronged, but they generally end up with the one they knew first. In the
case in point only Katona got the pick.

RING

The bride chooses the wedding ring. The groom pays for it then keeps
it till the day. It is traditional – and sometimes advisable – for the groom
to give it to the best man for safe keeping on the morning of the
wedding. The best man should then hand it back when they have taken
their places in the Church or Register Office.

USHERS

The ushers for the wedding are chosen by the bridegroom, and they tend to be chosen from among his close friends and/or the brothers of the bride. Their duties are not strictly defined, but it is usual to find them performing the following necessary functions on the wedding day:

Usher 1: hand out service sheets to the congregation at the church door. *(He may also be first reserve if the best man is indisposed, incapacitated or struck dumb with terror at the prospect of public speaking.)*

Usher 2: stand at the foot of the aisle and ask each guest 'bride or groom?' meaning whose friend or relative are they. According to their reply, they will be shown to a seat either on the left of the church (bride) or the right (groom). *(Holders of this office should be warned that there will inevitably be those who answer 'Both': such guests should be directed to the side of the church which at that moment contains fewer people.)*

Both Usher 1 and Usher 2 should try to keep the back rows of the church free for latecomers; they might also suggest aisle seats for guests with young children, so that they can leave unobtrusively if the infants get restless during the service.

Usher 3: stand halfway down the aisle to seat the guests. *(Not, you may rightly assume, a vital function, but a convenient job to give someone you feel needs something to do.)*

Usher 4: stand at the church door and escort the bride's mother to her seat on arrival. *(This may be incorporated into the job of Usher 1; alternatively, Usher 4 may also help Usher 1 hand out the service sheets.)*

Usher 5: organise parking of cars outside.

WHO PAYS

Since it is traditionally the bride's parents who pay for the wedding, they take the responsibility for organising the venue and the press announcement, if any. It is they who compile the guest list, naturally in consultation with the groom and his parents, and send out the invitations. They also foot the bill for the reception.

However, circumstances alter cases, and there is no suggestion that if the bride's lot cannot afford it all the marriage cannot go ahead: in realistic practical terms the money comes out of the account that can most easily sustain the withdrawals. Neither the groom nor his family should feel that it is a breach of etiquette to make a financial contribution.

SEPARATION AND DIVORCE

There is nothing like marriage: it is the only contract between two people that demands lifelong commitment regardless of changing circumstances, 'For richer, for poorer, for better, for worse'. It is so difficult that it should really not be shocking when it fails. But shocking it often is, and it is when people are taken unawares that they are most likely to say something tactless. So if a husband and wife announce that they are parting, remember never to say anything that may be construed as judgemental. Never express shock along the lines of 'I always thought you two were perfectly suited', and by the same token never say 'You'll be much happier now: I never did like him anyway'.

If you liked only one of the parties, the way forward is clear – drop the other like a stone. If you liked them both, you will in future have to consider the social consequences. If you have a party and invite them both, you will have to tell each that the other may be coming. This can be done by phone or in a note with the invitation.

In some cases – a very few – separation leads not to divorce but to reconciliation. So that's all the more reason to keep your views of the characters involved strictly to yourself.

The divorced couple need to be constantly mindful that if they are going to remain in the same social circles they must behave civilly to each other in public. Rowing in the plain view of one's friends is intolerable, and it is beyond the call of duty for your host to be expected to keep an eye on you both.

If a husband and wife decide to separate they should let all their relatives and friends know about it as quickly as they can. That doesn't always come easily – they are distraught and reluctant to discuss personal matters with outsiders – but it's a nettle that needs to be grasped. The information is often imparted in a note that accompanies the Christmas card: not ideal at the time of peace on Earth and good will to all men, but since many people only communicate in writing at this time of year I suppose there's little alternative. Certainly there are few people who will want to write personal letters on the subject to all their friends.

After a divorce, the woman may revert to her maiden name. More usually, however, she keeps her married surname but is henceforth known not as Mrs Henry Tudor but as Mrs Catharine Tudor. Which is just what she would do if she had been widowed.

You might want to try to pair off your newly divorced friend with someone you know to be available and whom you regard as suitable. While there is ample evidence that this sometimes works a treat, it is still better to tread carefully. Many divorced people have reported pitching up at social occasions where they know everyone present bar one, the purpose of whose presence is perfectly apparent from the moment of arrival.

Masculine intuition: he knew they were right for each other.

DEATH AND CONDOLENCE

The best expressions of sympathy – both written and spoken – show understanding of the relationship between the addressee and the dead person.

It is common for people who have lost loved ones to reproach themselves with thoughts that they might have done more for the deceased, that they should have been there for him when they were needed, and even that the death itself may somehow have been averted by their presence. Any happiness that the bereaved may have brought the deceased should therefore be emphasised as much as possible. It is good to say or write, if you can do so in good conscience, that the bereaved were indispensable to the dead person, that they improved the quality of his life, or even that they saw the deceased as much as possible during life.

It is also good to dwell on your own pleasant memories of the dead person – reminiscence is good, especially if it is a nice story which the addressee will not already know.

Anyone who has lost parents or siblings may fear that whatever killed them may also come for them. If you know of anything – debilitating childhood illness or graduate work with plutonium – which

HORSE SENSE?

At the funeral of Robin Cook in August 2005, television racing pundit John McCririck slated Tony Blair for not attending. He said: 'I believe the Prime Minister's snub to Robin's family, to millions of Labour voters, demonstrates a petty vindictiveness and moral failure, opting to continue snorkelling instead of doing his duty'. Even if the family marked his card, this is a lapse of taste – such remarks should be left in pickle and brought out to add flavour to the memoirs, unless wiser counsels have prevailed in the meantime.

might be taken as a fairly sure sign that history will not repeat itself, it were well to mention it.

Sympathetic people should try to ensure that the bereaved have plenty to occupy them and little opportunity to become even lower of spirit through excessive introspection.

BAD MEMORIES

If you knew something bad about the deceased and you didn't tell anyone about it in his lifetime, let him take your secret to the grave. The reminiscences that appear in the *Times* over the days following the main obituary invariably celebrate the qualities of the dead person; they do not dwell on his shortcomings, sins and outrages.

It is not acceptable to say that the deceased wasted his talent or that he was a good-for-nothing, especially if it's the truth.

LONG TERM PROGRESS

There is no need to depreciate death. The bereaved are not St Paul, they do not believe it has no sting. As long as you speak from experience and with sympathy, it is permissible to say, for example, that the loss of a loved one will always hurt. At first, it will hurt every day; after a while it may be possible to go for a week without thinking about the loss; sooner or later the time may come when whole months pass without the dead person crossing your mind. Gradually, perspective and balance are largely restored, and sunny memories will peep through the clouds. But for the rest of your life, somewhere, sometime, often when you least expect it, a memory of that person's death will creep up and hurt you again. Thus do the dead take possession of the living.

SOCIAL EVENTS

This section deals principally with how a host should notify people of his forthcoming social functions, how guests should respond to invitations, and what preparations they need to make before they set out. It also has a couple of tips about how guests should conduct themselves at the event, and a sympathetic endnote about the difficulties of getting stuck with one person.

AT HOME

When this appears on an invitation, it means that you don't need to take a bottle of wine with you unless you are specifically asked to do so. Dress smartly.

BOTTLE PARTY

Bottle parties are for students. The drinks' table at any bottle party is filled with exactly the sort of wine that people take to other people's parties. Nevertheless, you are supposed to take a bottle to a bottle party. (If you think that this is too obvious to mention, you may never have thrown a bottle party of your own. In which case you have better taste than can reasonably be expected of you, given your youth and unworldliness.) It is not usual to take a bottle to an 'at home'.

COCKTAIL PARTY

A cocktail party is usually held in the early evening and can be almost anything the host wishes it to be. Although dinner will not be served, there may be 'nibbles' (canapés, sandwiches, small sausages and the like). The only rule is that cocktails are never served.

Invitations may be telephoned, but if they are printed or written they should say simply 'Cocktails 5–7' ('pm' may be added, but will be understood), together with the date of the party. They should also have 'R.S.V.P.' with the host's name, address and phone number in the bottom left hand corner of the card.

DANCING

Men have always been able to ask women to dance, but now women can ask men without embarrassment. If the person asked doesn't want to, he or she should not say 'No'. It were better to recall Proverbs 15, i, 'A soft answer turneth away wrath', and say something like 'I'd rather sit this one out, if you don't mind'.

GATECRASHING

If you have God-like understanding and forgiveness of your fellow men, you may not detest those who gatecrash your party – you may even take it as a compliment that they should wish to appear at a function they were not asked to attend. Most people are not so charitable. However, the temptation to say 'If I'd known you were coming, I'd have invited you' should be resisted – you will probably have to bite the bullet and pretend you're delighted to see them. If guests ask beforehand if they can bring so-and-so, feel free to say no – unless of course you want so-and-so and had simply forgotten him or didn't know he was in the country.

If someone you have invited turns up with someone else you have not, again you'll have to lump it, but you'll know who not to ask next time.

GIFTS

Whatever the occasion – birthday, wedding or anniversary – the ground rules are clear: try to give something the recipient will want, but if you can't think of anything, give something impressive and/or expensive. Still it's much the best course to give something useful or of personal significance, even if it costs very little.

Gift tokens are a good choice, even though they let the recipient know how much they cost. Some people think such presents show a lack of thought, but that is a mistake: a gift token for a famous store has cachet and carries no attendant danger of duplicating someone else's gift. The only proviso is that people who live in the Orkneys may not have much occasion to shop at Selfridges, so care has to be exercised over the proximity of the recipient to the shop.

If the hosts insist that they want nothing don't be annoyed, remember all the other invitations that evoked the unworthy thought that the people were just soliciting. In case you really want or feel you ought to give them a gift, make it something that will go in an envelope, which you can keep about your person – tickets to some event, perhaps. Then you can arrive empty-handed yet not feel uncomfortable. Alternatively you can send flowers (*qv*) to arrive just before or just after the event.

Although you should never normally arrive at a birthday party without a present, at lunches and dinner parties the form is different and more complicated and most visitors will feel more at ease if they do not enter the house empty-handed. If you can't think of anything particularly apt for the occasion, that is where chocolates or flowers come in.

To those who have everything, give flowers. For children you love but don't know, money may be better than an irrelevance. If you send flowers or a present to a wedding you don't attend and you never get an acknowledgement, you should come out with it and ask, they may have been lost in the post or the shop from which you ordered them may have made a mistake.

RECEIVING GIFTS

When presented with gifts, the hostess should quickly take a view on what to do with them. If they're obviously edible or drinkable, she should put them close by to be served at the appropriate moment – chocolates, for example, should be served after dinner. If she's been presented with a very good wine, she should ask the guest what he wants done with it – should I drink it now, or save it for when I'm alone?

(A good guest will endeavour to answer this question before it is asked.) In the case of flowers, it is probably better not to flap around arranging them there and then, but to stick them in the nearest vase or sink and put them out only after everyone has gone home. If it's a personal gift the giver should suggest that the recipient might like to open it later. By the same token, if the size of the gift puts the recipient in fear that she will have to spend half an hour unwrapping, cooing and thanking – time better spent on getting the evening going and serving the food – she should say 'Thanks, do you mind if I open it later?' and pop it away.

'You think you're getting dinner, don't you?

WINE

Guests above a certain age (typically, those who are older than university students or those beyond their first job) need not take bottles of wine to parties (*but see Bottle Party, page 158*). There is no rule about this – if you've got some particularly toothsome vintage you wish to share, don't be inhibited. But it's better to take no wine than a bottle of something cheap and nasty.

Hosts are expected to be able to afford their own booze, their tastes may be different from yours and the wine you choose may not be appropriate for the meal. In some countries it's regarded as an insult to take wine because to do so implies that the hostess can't be relied upon to organise such things herself.

INVITATIONS

It is tactful and wise not to put invitations you have received on the mantelpiece or anywhere they are likely to be seen by mutual friends who may not have been asked.

If your children do not appear on the invitation, you may take it that they are not invited and that it is a violation of etiquette to ring up and ask the host for clarification of this point.

ADVANCED WARNING

If you are holding any sort of do, it is important to get the length of notice about right. If you give too much, the guests may think it's a very grand affair; moreover they might forget about it in the intervening period. If you give too little warning you may cause offence to those who think they're just emergency fill-ins. You may give people longer to make up their minds in certain circumstances, especially if the proposed function is to be held during a peak holiday period.

The rules of thumb are as follows:

- people you don't know very well should be given about a fortnight's notice.

- strangers or VIPs or busy people should be allowed longer, perhaps as long as a month.

- close friends need no notice, but don't push your luck.

WORDING AN INVITATION

Printed invitations may be styled in the third person — for example:

Mr and Mrs Jacob Primley request the pleasure of your company at a party to celebrate

Lucy's birthday

The Langham Hotel, London W1
Saturday 4th July, 7.30 pm
Black tie

RSVP

The legend should give the occasion (Lucy's birthday), the location (The Langham), the date and the time. Don't forget to mention any dress requirements. The name of the recipient should be written by hand in the top left-hand corner of the card.

———— ❧ ————

INVITATION CARDS

In this unbuttoned age, it no longer much matters whether invitation cards to 'at homes' (*see page 158*) and Weddings (*see page 144*) are printed or engraved. Nevertheless, sticklers for convention prefer engraved cards, these are more expensive but look more impressive. Invitation cards were once addressed to the wife, but that is no longer necessary. (Sympathy cards, incidentally, need not be black-edged.)

———— ❧ ————

PLUSES

Some party throwers write 'John Smith plus one' (alternatively '+1'), or 'plus friend' or 'and family'. The absence of such addenda means that John Smith should pitch up alone. Some people disapprove of '+1' on the grounds of impersonality: if you don't know the name, don't invite the person, even if it is a good friend of a friend. However, this only applies to formal, grown-up dos, if you're having a bottle party (*see page 158*) or some other casual bash, '+1' is fine. It is also fine if the person you're inviting is likely to change companions without you necessarily being up-to-date with the latest developments.

———— ❧ ————

MINUSES

Instead of RSVP, some invitations say 'Regrets only'. So if you are going, you can put the money you saved by not having to reply to the host into a better present...

LEAVING

How long are guests expected to stay at a function? This can sometimes be stated on the invitation without causing offence. It is not rude to put '6.30–8.00' it is just cultural shorthand for 'Dinner will not be served'. Normally, lunch should be over by 3 pm, dinner guests should make noises about leaving at about 11.30 pm and aim to be out of the door by midnight unless they are pressed to stay.

Loads of people fall asleep the first time they hear that story…

LOYAL TOAST

The loyal toast is a toast to the Queen, and consists of the toastmaster raising his glass and saying, simply, '(My Lords), Ladies and Gentlemen: The Queen'. If there is a second loyal toast it will be to 'The Prince Philip, Duke of Edinburgh, The Prince of Wales and the other Members of the Royal Family'. After the loyal toast or toasts, the guests may smoke. Therefore 'You may now smoke if you wish' is redundant, the phrase was more suited to 20th-century aircraft cabins than high-grade dinners. The exception to this is dinners at which the Queen herself is present, here the announcement should be, 'Ladies and Gentlemen, you have Her Majesty's permission to smoke'.

MUSIC

No matter how great the temptation to use music at social functions as an ice-breaker, to cover silences or dampen the sounds of punch-ups and rampant petomanes, it should not be played as background for a formal occasion, especially a formal meal. If it's good music, it should be listened to with full attention, if it's not good music it should not be heard at all.

SEATING PLAN

One of the host's greatest advantages is that he can fix the seating plan to ensure that he is next to the most interesting guest and as far as possible away from the biggest bore. Apart from that, the main rule is, to keep husbands and wives apart at the table. Some authorities say that lovers should be seated next to each other, but experience dictates that it is better to treat such couples as married than to have them feeling each other up under the table while you're trying to scintillate the assembly with your repartee. The most important male guest should be seated on the hostess's right, and the most important female should be placed on the right of the host. Thence it should be man–woman–man–woman around the table.

VISITING

After ringing the doorbell, it is conventional to get off the doorstep and wait there until someone answers. (Just one step, that is, if the entrance is at the top of a flight, you are not expected to beat the retreat.) This is a wise course of action in case the householder should spring out at you like a Jack-in-the-box with a clenched fist or offensive weapon. In earlier times, callers would keep their distance to avoid attack by castellans who might pour boiling oil from the battlements onto the heads of the medieval equivalents of encyclopaedia salesmen and Jehovah's Witnesses.

At a large dinner party you will usually talk to the person seated on your immediate left or right. In the happy event that you find each other agreeable and talk until the end of the main course, remember the guest on your other side and talk to him during the pudding.

If you are expected to change seats for pudding, talk to one side during the starter and the other during the main. Unless, of course, either party is inextricably engrossed with the person on the far side.

Normally you shouldn't leave another guest on his own. But that only works if people circulate, and let's face it they seldom do. So if you get marooned, and you can't even wave to passing ships, you've just got to pretend that the person with whom you're stuck is the companion you would have chosen if you'd had a scintilla of free will. If no one comes to rescue you, your only hopes are if your mobile rings or if you really are in desperate need of the loo. But it has to be a real emergency.

TECHNIQUETTE

It was from Bobby Ewing, a character in *Dallas*, a popular television series of the late 1970s and early 1980s, that I first heard the axiom 'Conversation is a two-way street'. Since actor Patrick Duffy delivered that daft but evidently memorable line, the thoroughfare to which he referred has been widened into a multi-lane superhighway by a technological revolution that has made mobile phones, e-mail and Blackberries part of many people's everyday lives. Such innovations have raised various new questions of etiquette.

ANSWERING MACHINES/ VOICEMAIL

It is a violation of etiquette to ring and not leave a message. The sole exception to this rule is in cases where you have got a wrong number. An even worse fault is to leave a message when you know before you call that the other person is going to be out and then assume that the onus is on him to get back to you. It may keep the phone bill down, but it's mighty annoying.

It is maddening to have to listen to recorded messages that are supposed to be funny. One irritating young man formerly of my acquaintance taped part of Edvard Grieg's incidental music for *Peer Gynt* over which he was to be heard saying 'This is the Hall of the Mountain King. I'm afraid the Mountain King is not available at the moment…'.

E-MAIL

First pick your weapon: should you write a letter, send an e-mail, make a phone call, or set up a meeting?

If you've decided to put whatever it is in writing, you've then got to choose letter or e-mail. If you're replying, you will generally respond by the same method as that in which you were contacted, but if you're initiating the correspondence, it's a matter for you.

If you decide it's to be a letter, you or your employer will almost certainly have a template – address ranged left, ranged right, whatever. Letter etiquette is dealt with elsewhere (*see Forms of Address, particularly page 46*), and a lot of the lessons of e-mail are equally applicable to traditional correspondence.

E-mail is full of traps, not the least of which is that it is superficially a more informal medium than the traditional paper letter. Many people send each other dirty jokes and rude attachments electronically, not only from their own PCs but also through work. If you are not certain that such material will be welcomed, don't send it.

Be on your guard about what you write and the way you express yourself. Letters begin with 'Dear So-and-So' and end with 'Yours faithfully' or 'Yours sincerely', e-mails typically begin with 'Hi' but that doesn't mean that the person addressed is your best mate, or would ever want to be. They normally end with just the name of the sender, and sometimes not even that, because it is after all on the top line. You can use a valediction if you wish, but it's neither usual nor expected.

Informal e-mails can be as informal as you like or think you can get away with, but business e-mails should stick to the rules of normal, old-style paper correspondence: let them begin with 'Dear So-and-so' and end with 'Yours sincerely', 'Yours faithfully', 'Best wishes', 'Yours truly' or whatever.

Never make the mistake of thinking that e-mail is private. Be careful what you say, and be ever mindful of the ease with which rude remarks can be forwarded – accidentally or accidentally on purpose – to the person being insulted.

Opening the attachment in an open plan office was probably a mistake.

STRINGS OF INITIALS

Don't use abbreviations such as 'AFAIK' (as far as I know) 'OTOH' (on the other hand), 'IYAM' (if you ask me) and so on, they're not clever and they're not smart, they're just annoying to those who don't know what they mean and boring to those who do. They're okay on SMS (text messages), but nowhere else.

TEXT ABBREVIATIONS

You get a message and it's full of abbreviations that you don't understand. Is the sender rudely presumptuous, or are you thick and Luddite? I don't know the answer to that, but these are some of the most commonly used groups of initials whose meaning may not immediately be obvious to the uninitiated.

aml	all my love
atm	at the moment
bbl	be back later
brb	be right back
btw	by the way
cul8r	see you later
fyeo	for your eyes only
hwc	handle with care
lol	lots of love (or laugh out loud: context is all)
oic	oh I see
omg	oh my God
rofl	rolling on the floor laughing
soz	sorry
tb	text back
tbs	text back soon
ttyl	talk to you later
tx	thanks
umbj	you must be joking

AUTOMATIC REPLIES

Templates for frequently used responses can save you a lot of time and effort, but they may annoy those who receive them. It is in general better to keep someone waiting a week for a full and considered answer to his queries or problems than to send a 'Thank you for your communication' type reply. Most people have great confidence in e-mail – if they send a message and it doesn't get returned, they assume it's got through. Automatic 'out of the office' responses can get trapped in a loop – two machines tell each other a thousand times that the query will be dealt with on their users' return from holiday.

If you need to attach files, tread carefully – it's often better to check if the intended recipient can read the program you're thinking of sending than to unleash a dirty great document that may take half an hour to download and then be unopenable.

Don't tie yourself in knots about gender neutral language. Some people are offended by the use of masculine pronouns when they may refer to females. Hence a sentence such as 'All we are asking is that every child should learn from his experience' may be changed to 'All we are asking is that every child should learn from his or her experience'. The problem with that is that the user ends up having to mention both sexes in all his/her writing, ending up with a page full of forward slashes that may end up driving him/her wo/mental. The elegant way out of this is to use the plural passim: 'All we are asking is that children should learn from experience'.

Mind your language, and bear in mind that some companies have filters that will refuse anything deemed to be potentially offensive: I had an e-mail bounced back from a very straight-laced company because the correspondence referred to a football club named Arsenal. If I'd written about Scunthorpe United, would they have called the police?

Avoid in-house jargon for members of the public: you may call your Ways and Means Building Organisation by the acronym WAMBO, but it's unfair to expect anyone outside the company to know what you're going on about.

If you are tempted to incorporate any of the letters which you may be entitled to put after your name into your e-mail address, resist with every ounce of strength at your disposal: 'shipmanmd', 'rideauxqc' and 'haythornthwaitekcmg' are quite beyond the pale.

OTHER NETIQUETTE RULES

• Don't use the exclamation mark high-priority flag as a matter of course.

• Avoid the use of block capitals, PEOPLE SAY IT'S SHOUTING. Exclamation marks are also to be avoided, as they are in real letters.

• Check what's written on the subject line, if it really is a reply, leave in the 'Re:' if it's to the same person but about something else, put in a new header.

• Add disclaimers that make it clear that not everything written by an employee is company policy.

• Think about cc-ing and replying to all, do they really need to know this?

• Be careful about forwarding a message, does the person to whom you're intending to send it really want or need to know?

• Don't forward chain letters about ways of getting money out of Bill Gates and fortunes from frozen bank accounts in Nigeria.

• Warnings about viruses are seldom useful and usually extremely boring.

• Don't e-mail confidential material: write a proper letter or arrange a meeting.

• Don't let the spell-check fool you into avoiding the passive voice, if he was killed, how else do you say it?

MOBILE TELEPHONES

If a person has only one phone and that phone is a mobile, it is difficult to adduce cogent reasons why he should not make and receive calls in public places as well as at home. However, it is aesthetically repugnant to have to endure the sight and sound of people using mobiles in any milieu which, but for their presence, would be perfectly unblighted by the telephone. A telephone conversation is a form of intimacy, not a spectator sport. It is regrettable that some people take and make mobile telephone calls in public in an attempt to show the uninterested world how busy and important they are. As for people who let them ring during theatrical performances, there is no fate too awful.

If you're going into a meeting or a cinema or a theatre you will of course switch your mobile off at the entrance. But in restaurants most people leave them on. While the mobile was still new-fangled I did

'I wouldn't mind, but it's an answering machine she's talking too.'

wonder how bad it would be to answer mine at lunch it if it rang and the display showed the name of anyone other than a caller of the highest conceivable importance. But since then I've been to so many such events at which fellow diners have taken calls that I've become convinced that it is not a heinous thing to do. Certainly I've never been offended. All you need to do is avoid making calls yourself, and ensure that you spend more than half the time at the table concentrating on the corporeal presences that are with you.

The only real objection to the use of mobile phones on public transport is the low quality of the ensuing dialogue. It's not that one expects a torrent of epigrams, merely that, even as statements of the obvious go, 'I'm on a train' is dramatic irony of the lowest imaginable order. And it would help if they didn't talk like they were making a public announcement.

AN ACTOR DESPAIRS

In 2004, actor Richard Griffiths responded angrily to a member of the audience whose phone had gone off six times during a performance of *The History Boys* at The National Theatre. He came to the front of the stage, pointed at the perpetrator, and told him: 'Go, and never come back'. In November 2005, he rose again after a phone rang in the audience for the third time during a performance of *Heroes* at the Wyndham's Theatre. He stepped out of part and demanded: 'Is that it, or will it be ringing some more?' Warming to his theme, he reportedly continued, 'Could the person whose mobile it is please leave? The 750 people here would be fully justified in suing you for ruining their afternoon'.

OHRWURMEN

If you suddenly find that a snatch of music has lodged itself unaccountably in your brain and will not be banished – a phenomenon that Germans call an 'earworm' – you may well have got it from someone else's mobile phone ring tone. After a decade of the Overture to Bizet's *Carmen*, 'La donna é mobile' from Verdi's *Rigoletto* and others, there are now welcome signs of a long overdue backlash against such irritating tunes. Despite the fact that some people have downloaded the Crazy Frog jingle, others – the cultural elite? – have adopted the tone of the old traditional Bakelite phone in the hall. So there's hope of peace for the rest of us.

PA SYSTEMS

How soon do a microphone and a captive audience turn a normally harmless person into a homicidal bore? Remember that all art aspires to the condition of music, not to that of disc jockeys, purveyors of what Geoffrey Grigson termed 'ponce-patter'.

TELEPHONE

It is incumbent upon the person who makes the call to be forthcoming with information first. Do not ring a number and immediately demand to know to whom you are speaking, it is up to you to identify yourself. If you're ringing A at B's house and B answers the phone, it is as well to sound apologetic about bothering him. Keep any messages you may wish to leave with B for A short.

When you answer your own phone say 'Hello'. If you're especially benevolent you might say the number, but why should you when it might be a heavy breather who's misdialled and likes the sound of your voice? If someone rings you and says 'Is that 012-3456-7890?' and it isn't, that is all they need to be told, they do not need to know your correct number.

If a caller asks to speak to someone other than yourself, normally the polite thing to do is to hand the phone over immediately to the person requested. If, on the other hand, you have the job of fielding calls for someone who will speak to caller A but doesn't want to hear from caller B, you may have to find out the caller's name.

'*May I ask who's calling?*'

is the perfect form of words.

'*May I ask what it's about?*'

however, is nosey and invites a flea in the ear.

Anyone unfortunate enough to be asked this impertinent question should politely deflect it by saying 'It's a personal matter'. This response will do even if it's obviously a business call and you've never met whoever it is.

If you're a guest in someone's home and you need to use his phone, ask for permission first.

MISSED A CALL?

You miss a call; you dial the "last number" function (1471); you don't recognise it; you ring the caller. What do you say when you get an answer? Your own name and "did you just ring me?" If you omit the former you're inviting the response "I don't know, who are you?" and thus in a trice you're on a war footing before you realise it's your oldest friend from an unfamiliar phone.

LET YOUR OWN FINGERS DO THE WALKING

At work, dial your calls yourself – don't instruct underlings to do it for you. In some firms it is regarded as good practice to say your own name when you pick up the receiver. While that seems unnatural to me – why should you give away such precious information before you know whether you're dealing with a friend or a foe? – I have never worked for anyone who insisted on it, and if I had I am sure I would just have done as I was asked.

FANCY A CHAT?

Even if you've got time to kill shooting the breeze down the phone, don't assume that the other person is at a similarly loose end. Ask if now is a good time. And even if you get an affirmative response, don't jump to the conclusion that he is up for the full 140 minutes.

UNSOLICITED PHONE CALLS FROM SALESMEN

Some people say that you should tolerate the heaving of such rocks into the pool of your domestic tranquillity at the most inconvenient times (just as the joint is being carved for a Sunday lunch) since most of the callers are impoverished youths trying to make an honest buck. While torrents of abuse are discourteous and do not in my experience even get your number removed from their lists, it is surely no bad thing to say 'Not interested' and put the phone down. If call centres did not exist, it would not be necessary to invent them, and students would find other ways of eking out their grants.

MISCELLANEOUS

This chapter includes manners for discussion that would appear on a meeting agenda under the heading Any Other Business. The topics are neither more nor less important than the other material in this book; they have merely proved harder to categorise. Again the reader may either follow the guidelines or scoff at the very idea of them. But if you take the latter course you should be aware that some people set great store by such rules and may judge you on your choices. If you don't care about any of that, fair play to you as they say in Ireland: just so long as you know that you'll be branded by some as a wild card or a dissident.

CHARITY

We all want to do good, even if only for our own sakes. Those of us who have more than we require may want to redirect some of the surplus towards the less fortunate. It is then that the problems start.

REASONS FOR GIVING TO CHARITY

1. Selflessness, or perhaps even pathological generosity
An excessive awareness that we come naked into the world and go out of it in the same state, which nurtures a disinclination to be well-heeled during the intervening span.

2. Guilt
When we see a tramp, meet the victim of a debilitating illness or read about a natural disaster, we think 'There but for the grace of God go I'.

3. Enlightened self-interest
This may be commixed with or even disguised as sentiment – if generations of your same-sex forebears have pegged out through myocardial infarction, you may regard donations to the British Heart Foundation as wise investments.

4. Tax planning
Some gifts to charity may be offset against the total amount owed to the state.

5. Self-gratification
You may not give a fig for the Chesterfield Fund for the Alleviation of Rheumatism, but you like its quiz nights and wine-tasting evenings so much that you are prepared to pay the inflated ticket prices.

REASONS FOR NOT GIVING TO CHARITY

1. Pure selfishness
No time, nothing to spare, sod them all.

2. This is a dog-eat-dog world
Sauve qui peut / heaven only helps those who help themselves / if you give a man a meal you are not helping him to feed himself.

3. Fear that the money does not reach those in need
That your donations will not reach the intended recipients, instead, they might be swallowed up by administration costs and the charities' executives' salaries.

4. Embarrassment of choice
How can one take the part of one charity over another? They're all worthy, so it is invidious to support the Great Ormond Street Hospital and give nothing to Cystic Fibrosis.

5. Charity begins at home
If we give promiscuously to unidentified strangers, we are no better than Mrs Jellyby, the 'telescopic philanthropist' in Dickens' *Bleak House*.

AGAINST DIRECT ACTION

If you want to help but fear Point 3 in Table 2, you could just give money directly to worthy-looking individuals. Jesus Christ said: 'Love your neighbour as yourself', but Norman Douglas wondered 'Now what has that gentleman done to deserve our love?'

The gentleman himself may ask the same question: the beggar who asks passers-by to spare him the price of a cup of tea may not take kindly to being frogmarched off to the nearest cafe.

COMMUNAL LIVING

FLAT SHARING

1) Pay your share in full and on time.

2) Don't take the last of anything without replacing it immediately.

3) Rinse the bath after use.

4) Put everything back where you found it.

5) Regard your flatmates' bedrooms as inviolable sanctuaries.

6) Leave everything – particularly the sink and the loo – as you would wish to find it.

7) Don't leave your impedimenta strewn around the common parts.

8) If you ignore Point 7, don't be resentful or harbour grudges when your stuff disappears or gets broken by a vandal whom you never identify.

9) Don't move your partner in as a full-time non-paying extra tenant.

10) Remember that the flat-sharing arrangement isn't permanent, drop anchor but don't take root.

DRIVING

There is little that needs to be added to *The Highway Code* (a readily obtainable, competitively priced and useful publication which, nevertheless, most road users would rather praise than read), save the wisdom of always bearing in mind that most people do not drive badly deliberately or maliciously. Don't bang on about women drivers, and don't complain that the lights are always against you: they're not, and over a lifetime it will all even out. Keep these few precepts in thy memory, and road rage will be avoided as easily as any sober lamppost.

THE HORN

Research shows that nought percent of traffic jams are cleared by sounding the horn.

Use only while your vehicle is moving and you need to warn other road users of your presence. Never sound your horn aggressively. You MUST NOT use your horn:

• while stationary on the road.

• when driving in a built-up area between the hours of 11.30 pm and 7.00 am except when another vehicle poses a danger.

Rule 92, *The Highway Code*

CARS

In a sane world a motor car would be nothing more than a means of transport. In the real one it is often the owner's personal statement. No one can quite hear what he is saying, but he is definitely trying to tell us something about his means, his status and, in extreme cases, his pudenda. Since a man's car may be admired, envied or deplored by his fellows, his choice is to some degree influenced by manners: how does he want to come across? Does he want to dominate the swelling scene or remain part of the backdrop?

Men and women of taste and discernment do not seek status symbols: they drive the car that most closely fulfils their requirements within their price bracket. But many people wish to impress and cow others with the cost, size and classiness of their 'autostable'. Others are afraid of being ridiculed by their friends for being seen in a jalopy – for all such persons, the choice of the right car – or, at least, the avoidance of the wrong one, is crucial to the preservation of *amour propre*.

Some motors move in and out of fashion more nimbly than ever they negotiate urban congestion, but many marques continually struggle to escape stereotyping. Any bore will tell you that Italian cars 'rot like pears'; it is conventional (although increasingly anachronistic) to deplore the build quality and image of Korean and Malaysian vehicles. Many cars, especially the Ford Focus and the Vauxhall Astra, are sneered at because they are considered 'reppy' (fit only to be driven by travelling salesmen).

You would be wise to be unimpressed by the level of debate on this subject. If, on the other hand, you are concerned to avoid being damned by association with your car, it may be worth noting some of the animadversions that follow.

Inverted snobs sometimes go for motorised tin cans that have some cachet because they are cheap and spartan. The East German Trabant, which was a two-stroke joke throughout its time as a production model, acquired great cachet as soon as it was discontinued after the collapse of Communism.

French cars tend to have more style than substance, and even their elegance may be vitiated by such idiosyncrasies as a foot-operated handbrake. German cars have few detractors, and most Porsches, Audis, Mercedes and Volkswagens are fit to grace driveways almost anywhere. Some Britons will still not buy them, however, because of the Second World War. There is a similar vestigial resistance to Japanese motors.

Journalists market themselves as wordsmiths, but many of them are secondary writers of the type thus described by Henri Douvray and quoted by Ezra Pound in The ABC of Reading: '*Ils cherchent des sentiments pour les accomoder à leur vocabulaire*'. That is the most benign explanation I can think of for the modern tendency of the motoring press to label as 'gay' any car that does not have six-speed cojones and a testosterone overdrive. The hacks are looking for an elegant variant for 'a woman's car', which they have decided, probably rightly, is more hackneyed than any carriage. But the alternative they have produced is needlessly offensive and descriptively none too evocative.

PERSONALISED NUMBER PLATES

These are acceptable in the United States but frowned on in Britain. If you really want people to know who you are, why don't you put your name on the windscreen and rear bumper rather than pay a premium for a registration plate that may be ostentatious, ludicrously contrived, or probably both?

A550 LE5

The earliest swanky number belonged to Earl Russell, who is reputed to have queued all night to secure the registration A1 for his Napier when plates were introduced in 1904. I once had to apply for a new number plate for a secondhand car I had purchased because the previous owner wanted to keep MRX something or other – I had to have it explained to me that it was 'Mr X'. More recently I have been offered such contrivances as RU55 ELL and SXE 1, but the marketing people never tried to sell me TO55 ER5, presumably because they wanted to keep it for themselves.

PUBLIC TRANSPORT

10 THINGS NOT TO DO ON PUBLIC TRANSPORT

1) Talk to the person next to you.

2) Touch anyone, no matter how crowded the conveyance.

3) Play music through headphones so loudly that others can hear it.

4) Eat: exceptions may be made for sweets, but recently microwaved meals are out of order, you are not in the restaurant car of The Orient Express.

5) Drop chewing gum or stick it on the furnishings.

6) Drink anything other than water or maybe tea or coffee from a thermos.

7) Sing.

8) Ask for money.

9) If you are male, sit with your legs spread so far apart that no one can comfortably occupy the adjacent seat.

10) Anything overtly sexual, alone or with others

SPORT

At the time of writing it is almost more likely that a Briton will not have a birth certificate than that he will claim no allegiance to some football club or another. For such partisanship to be socially acceptable, however, there has to be a good reason for it. One of the best validations is if your father supported, played for, or bankrolled the club you support. If you also had a grandparent with the same allegiance, that is impossible to trump. The club of one's native city is normally acceptable, too, although if the place has more than one team you will have to go an extra mile to gain the esteem of your peers: an Everton supporter, for example, will have to do a bit better than 'I was born in Kirkby' to avoid questions about what was wrong with Liverpool or even Tranmere Rovers.

If your club allegiance is neither inherited nor based on the place in which you were brought up, be aware that you may be giving away your age. Anyone who first got football as a child in the early Sixties may support Tottenham Hotspur because the team won the League and the FA Cup in the first year of that decade. West Ham United had a baby boom in the mid-Sixties, when they won major trophies in three consecutive years: the FA Cup in 1964, the European Cup Winners' Cup in 1965 and, in the view of their fans, the World Cup in 1966. Meanwhile recruitment to Arsenal colours slumped after 1953, when they entered the least successful period of their history. The drought lasted until 1971, when they emulated Spurs' Double achievement.

Before Manchester United became a world brand, they had surges of new support in 1958 in the wake of the Munich air disaster, and in 1968 when they became the first English club to win the European Cup.

An elderly or middle-aged Chelsea fan's support may be dated to either 1955, when they first won the League, or to 1970, when they beat Leeds United in a replayed FA Cup Final. Almost anyone who has come to them more recently – and particularly since they were bought by Roman Abramovich – is a nouveau, the kind of fan whom opposing supporters bait with chants of 'Where were you when you were shit? (You still are shit)'.

If you want to be really stylish, perhaps you should support nobody: be capable of conducting a conversation on the subject of football, but say you're non-partisan, just interested. No one expects anyone to support Warwickshire County Cricket Club, so why should zealotry of the 'If you cut my Wolverhampton wrist my blood would run old gold' type be regarded as the cynosure of cool?

KEEPING SPORT OUT OF POLITICS

Football has been 'sexy' in the 'technical' Ruud Gullit sense only since the advent of all-seater stadiums and Sky Television coverage, both of which began in the early 1990s. There was a time when men of mould would not have a team (or even if they did they would not prate of it) partly because it was not trendy, and partly because it revealed their working-class origins, which may have some advantages but are not for daily use. The perceived need to have a team is nowhere more revoltingly apparent than in the conduct of modern politicians. Before the Sixties, the only MP with a team was Harold Wilson, who made public his support for Huddersfield Town. Today they all seem to regard a club as an essential part of their electoral appeal. How wrong can they be?

Tony Blair is pilloried for saying that as a child at Newcastle United he sat in the Gallowgate End, which was then all terracing (standing-room only); Essex-born Jack Straw sounded a false note when, while speaking of 'his' Blackburn Rovers, whose ground happens to be in his parliamentary constituency, he described himself as 'a football enthusiast'.

AFTERWORD

'Another etiquette book? Who needs it?'

'Everyone.'

The author would say that, wouldn't he? But most works on the
subject are based on the assumption that good behaviour is
informed principally and perhaps exclusively by the conduct of the
upper classes. The premise is false. In his autobiography, Scouse
footballer Robbie Fowler said with reference to himself and fellow
England international Steve McManaman: 'When you come from
a council estate in Liverpool, how you come across is important.'

To anyone who thinks like that, regardless of class and education,
manners matter.

Also mistaken is the notion that only toffs are sufficiently civilised
to identify what Debrett's is fond of calling '*comme il faut*', and that
proles should learn from the aristocracy if they want to better
themselves.

Too many social commentators regard their job as prescriptive,
and their duty to right wrongs. Who asked them? On *Start The
Week,* presenter Andrew Marr introduced manners guru Peter
'Sloane Ranger Handbook' York as 'a style ayatollah'. The author
took it in good part, but it didn't sound like a compliment.

Few people want to be told what to do, they prefer broad
guidelines: etiquette's a jam session, not an obbligato, so I hope
you've treated this book as such.